CHOPPERS & ROAD TRIPS

By

Shovelhead Dave

Copyright © 2022 Shovelhead Dave

All rights reserved. No part of this book may be reproduced, stored, or transmitted by any means—whether auditory, graphic, mechanical, or electronic—without written permission of both publisher and author, except in the case of brief excerpts used in critical articles and reviews. Unauthorised reproduction of any part of this work is illegal and is punishable by law.

Printed and bound in Great Britain by
www.elitepublishingacademy.com

A catalogue record for this book
is available from The British Library

ISBN Paperback - 978-1-915730-00-8
ISBN eBook - 978-1-915730-01-5

FOREWORD

Finally, a totally different motorcycle book has been written. With this novel, you can step back in time to 1973 when a then 18 year old Shovelhead Dave didn't even have his 1974 Shovelhead yet. He was on a 1967 Sportster which he rode from Dallas Texas to Calgary Alberta, a road trip over 4,000 miles, with his cousin on a new 4 Cylinder Honda. How many 18-year-olds have done that? Incredible vintage photos of that trip are in this book.

In 1974, your author Dave becomes Shovelhead Dave when he gets the 1974 AMF Strike Built Shovelhead he still rides today, nearly 50 years later. He continues his long cross country camping road trips throughout the 1970s. There are plenty of vintage photos to feast your eyes upon. There is also a 1975 multi western state road trip with his brother on a Shovelhead and their cousin on his Norton Commando.

In the fall of 1975, Shovelhead Dave joins the "Build What You Ride, Ride What You Build" crowd by building his first rigid frame chopper and gets accepted into the underground Dallas- Fort Worth chopper crowd who rode choppers in the 1960s. The next five versions of Dave's chopper builds are included in this book.

Dave rides with the Dallas ABATE group to Daytona Bike Week in 1977 and gets involved in breakdowns on the road, his chopper catches on fire, it crashes, there are broken bones, and he gets busted out of a hospital. You might enjoy all the mayhem in this book if you are into old 1970s scooter trash life. Through the camera lens, you watch an 18 year old motorcycle boy turn into a 24 year old motorcycle man, and his trusty Shovelhead is a passion he keeps for life.

Brother Charles: 1975 the day after my high school graduation Brother Dave, Cousin John and I got on our bikes and hit the road ing me to use his old photo of his classic Knucklehead he's sittin' on at the KOA Kampground in New Smyrna Beach with Stan and Possum.

So here's to raising a glass and saying 'Cheers' to all you fun motorsickle crazies who made the zaniness happen. Without you guys ridin' along beside me, it never woulda been the same.

Memoirs by my baby brother Charles and cuzzin Johnny
Brother Charles

1975 the day after my high school graduation Brother Dave, Cousin John and I got on our bikes and hit the road for adventure. We headed out to see things and places we had only heard of. We saw so much more along the way, most of the time guided by a map and others by the weather. All while experiencing laughter, excitement, joy, fright, wonderment all in this beautiful land we live in. What fun it was and what memories we made.

Cuzzin Johnny:

Dave made the remark to me a couple of years ago, "Ya know, we were out on the road, just going where we decided to go, some-times sleeping in great hotels, sometimes sleeping out in the great outdoors, seeing this grand country, we were RICH, and didn't even know it." Great memories Cuz.

Spring of 1973

When I turned 18 in 1973 and became legally old enough to buy a motor vehicle on my own, instead of getting some boring car like some of my high school friends did, I went against my dad's orders and got this instead. It's a 1967 Sportster XLH, complete with windshield and saddlebags. Not exactly the vision I had for my own version of "Then Came Bronson" but it was close. I rode it from Dallas Texas to Ardmore Oklahoma which was 100 miles away for a test run. After that? I knew I was ready to take off to Calgary Alberta, hahaha, cuz umm,…why not? These are my first motorsickle photos ever and in a coat and tie yet I was ridin' to my buddy's wedding.

SHOVELHEAD DAVE

Spring 1973, just before we left on the Calgary Alberta Road Trip. I stripped the 67 Sportster XLH bagger stuff down to a more 'Then Came Bronson'-looking ride. And yes, I know the shirt, pants and shoes are goofy and nuts. It was 1973 and I was 18, so gimme a break.

THE EARLY YEARS

OK folks, before there was such a smelly critter as Shovelhead Dave back in 1974, there was the 18 year old Sportster Dave in 1973, on a used 1967 Red Sportster XLH. I loved the Easy Rider movie and Then Came Bronson on TV and knew that would be my life. So, for my high school grad-u-ma-ga-shun present to my own damn self, against everyone's opinion I took this road trip from Dallas to Calgary Alberta. My Cuzzin Paul rode along and luckily, he had a really nice camera and took all these 35 mm pictures, or I wouldn't have nuthin' to remember the trip by. So here we go, another road trip from Days Gone By.

1973 Cross Country Trip from Dallas to Canada

Part 1

I was 18, just out of high school and was wanting to do my own "Then Came Bronson" cross country road trip on my 1967 Sportster.

At first I planned to go solo, but then a week before I left, my 21 year old cuzzin wanted to ride along on his new 4 cylinder Honda, so there were 2 of us. Luckily my cuzzin Paul was a good photographer, otherwise I woulda never had these pictures of that fun road trip from Dallas, Texas to Calgary, Alberta. A little over 4,000 miles round trip,...which = sore butt.

Then a coupla days before we were scheduled to leave, Paul called up and said he had a friend who wanted to ride along. OK, no big deal. The day before we were supposed to leave, he called up and said his friend's brother wanted to go, hah. I said OK, but that's it, no more additions.

This is our starting point, in the Dallas driveway. Then we left Dallas and headed over to Fort Worth to pick up the other two guys who happened to be brothers, then we headed out Highway 287 toward the Panhandle.

Here is where the first "problem" happened. The other two guys with us were on little itty-bitty bikes, like Honda 350 little. When I first saw them, I asked Paul, "Are you sure these two guys can make it to Canada on those bikes?" He said he thought so, so off we went up Highway 287.

THE EARLY YEARS

After we had gone maybe 30 miles or so, they wanted to pull off the highway into a gas station to get gas. I was like what the fuck, didn't you even fill up your tanks before we left, hahaha? And as we pulled into the gas station, the oldest brother stood up from his Honda seat, stretched his legs and said, "Wow, that is the longest I ever rode in one sitting." I knew right then we were in trouble.

Now, at 18, I was the youngest guy in this group. My cousin Paul was 21 and one of the guys was 21 and the other one was 23, and it was the oldest guy in the group that had never ridden anywhere before.

I may have been only 18 and I was on a used 1967 Sportster instead of a new bike like all of theirs were, but at least I had ridden from Dallas into Oklahoma and Arkansas and over to New Braunfels as little warm up trips for this Long Road Trip. So, we filled the four gas tanks and were off to Palo Duro Canyon, next excitin' stop.

1973 Cross Country Trip from Dallas to Canada

Part 2

We left off last semi thrilling episode with the four of us punk kids riding motorsickles headed to Canada from Dallas. My Cuzzin Paul on his Honda 550 and me on the 67 Sportster picked up two brothers in Fort Worth and proceeded on toward Palo Duro Canyon outside Amarillo. Now if you old timers remember, the speed limit back in 1973 was 55 mph. I was wanting to cruise around 63 or so, but the two new guys on their little 350 Hondas could not do that very well.

I don't mean to be rude, but those two guys were really cramping my style, bwahahaha. Those 350s were not road bikes, they were ride around town bikes. Anyhow we managed to make it to Palo Duro Canyon that evening. It was a big hot dry dusty hole in the ground. How exciting, wink, wink.

We camped for the night next to the big hole in the ground. So far we had ridden a grand total of about 6 hours, and those two new guys were done for the night. Not good. They were whining about how sore their widdle butts were, and here they are in their 20s and I'm the 18-year-old? I should be the one whining, not them, hahaha.

This was the trip that introduced me to the wonders of KOA Kampgrounds, I loved those places. They had little road atlases they gave you, showing all the KOAs in the USA. When you were ready to pack it up and leave the next morning, you could talk to the guy in the office and tell him you planned on 400 or 500 miles, or whatever you felt like riding and sometimes that depended on weather conditions, too, and he could look that many miles ahead, find the KOA in that area, call them, and make a reservation for you. Bam! Just like that.

Who could ask for anything more? KOAs had nice campgrounds, showers, usually a joint to eat grub and a place to wash your dirty road clothes if you so desired, and sometimes, if you were really lucky, they'd have a swimming pool. We camped out that night outside Amarillo-Palo Duro area and packed it up the next morning and headed on our merry way. Riding 3 hours or so put us by Clayton New Mexico, then we rode on acrost the corner of New Mexico into Colorado.

Cuzzin Paul and I had a sweet gal Cuzzin Peggy that lived in Colorado Springs, kinda at the base of Pikes Peak and we were gonna see her this trip. This photo here is the ol' 67 Sportster and me at the New Mexico border.

1973 Cross Country Trip from Dallas to Canada

Part 3

We left off last time breaking camp by the Palo Duro Canyon outside Amarillo and headed on into New Mexico, Canada the destination. After ridin' through Clayton, we had roughly a 4 hour ride to Colorado Springs where Paul's and my Cuzzin Peggy lived. We made it with nothing bad happening, but the two little Honda 350 bikes were having trouble keeping up.

Now I ain't making fun of those little bikes, cuz I will give credit to the 2 brothers riding with us for even making it that far. I mean, who among us would start out from Fort Worth headed to Canada on a Honda 350? I know I sure as hell wouldn't have the guts to try it, hahaha. And in the beginning, I was wondering if my Cuzzin Paul's 550 was enough muscle to make the haul.

Seems Paul and I were always riding out front with the 2 little bikes trying to keep up and it was difficult making any good time that way, but that was what we had going on.

Anyhow we finally made it to our Cuzzin Peggy's apartment and we messed around her neighborhood some and threw our sleeping bags on her living room floor that night.

The next day was to be our Ride up Pikes Peak, 14,110 feet elevation. I was wondering how the Honda 350s would take that ride.

So, we got to the base of the mountain and headed up The Big Hill. Peggy hopped on the back of Paul's Honda 550, mainly because it was a brand-new bike and who woulda thought a 6-year-old used 1967 Sportster would make it up that big hill. As we got maybe halfway up Pikes Peak, trouble was looming on the horizon for the Hondas, all 3 of the Hondas. The little bikes were lacking the torque to make the big pull, but they kept huffing and puffing along.

Paul's brand-new Honda 550, on the other hand, had another problem. Or maybe I should say four problems, as in, those four carbs, all synchronized for Dallas elevation air. The higher we went up, the less air there was…see? And those 4 carbs on the 550 kept shoveling in the same amount of gas as if they were at ground level, so that new 550 was blowing black smoke out all 4 tail pipes, losing energy.

At this level, we pulled over to rest the Hondas, and Peggy decided she would ride the rest of the way up with me, like she shoulda done in the first place. But I was the 18-year-old kid, so who was I to tell the "adults" what to do?

That 67 Sportster still had the stock Tillotson carb on it. And it had that diaphragm in it, and the less air there was, the less gas it took in. That Ironhead 67 still had plenty of power even over 10,000 feet elevation. It hauled Peggy and me right up to the summit like it was no big deal, and the Hondas came huffing and puffing up after us a few minutes later. I remember watching them make the final bend, black smoke billowing out all those exhaust pipes.

I tried explaining to the Honda Guys, "Hey, I ain't meanin' to be rude running off and leaving you guys like that, but I gotta keep the air flowing over this old motor or it will heat up bad."

After all, it is an Ironhead,…right? This photo taken by Cuzzin Paul is where we took a break about half way up Pikes Peak, where Peggy got off the new Honda 550 and got herself on the 6-year-old Ironhead.

SHOVELHEAD DAVE

1973 Cross Country Trip from Dallas to Canada

Part 4

We left off last time with the 67 Sportster up on top of Pikes Peak where it had hauled my Cuzzin Peggy and me up the 14,110 feet. The 3 Hondas came up a little bit later, billowing black smoke, but all was well at the summit. The Tillotson carb on the 67 Sportster was a diaphragm type carb and when it got into less air, it simply took in less gas. But the Hondas had synchronized carbs and were set for ground elevation. But the Hondas did make it to the top, so that was good. We stayed up on the summit for a while, then rode back down. The Hondas seemed to like going downhill better than up, hah. When we got to the bottom, there was a place we ate at in Manitou Springs, the town next to the base of Pikes Peak.

The group of us went in to eat vittels and when we came back out, some low life sum-bitch had stolen my Levi jacket off the back pack on the Sportster. It was the only jacket I had with me, and it had the kool ass Harley wings on the back, and now it was gone. Muthafucker! And no, it didn't fall off somewhere cuz I had it tied in there good, and somebody undid the bungee cords and took it. So now I had to get another jacket to wear for the rest of the trip since it was going to be mostly mountainous high country from here on out.

There was a tourist type shop across the street from the restaurant, so I moseyed on over there and found the Pioneer jacket I still have all these years later. It is a buckskin fringe, sorta like the one Billy wears in Easy Rider, so that leather fringe became my new jacket and pillow for camping, multi-tasking in 1973.

SHOVELHEAD DAVE

Next up on the agenda, we rode over to Canon City where the Royal Gorge Bridge is and a place that was called Buckskin Joe's, an old cowboy town with real dirt streets and old buildings where they filmed Cat Balou, which was made in 1965 and John Wayne's movie The Cowboys which was made in 1972 and other old western movies. We got 3 photos here, 1 from Buckskin Joe's and the other 2 photos are on Pikes Peak, one looking down at then-little Colorado Springs back in 1973, the other one is of us riders on the side of the road.

THE EARLY YEARS

1973 Cross Country Trip from Dallas to Canada

Part 5

Last time we left off riding down from Pikes Peak, stopping in at Manitou Springs for grub, then coming out to discover some ass wipe had ripped off my Levi jacket, the only jacket I had, so I went across the street and got a brand-new leather fringe jacket kinda like Billy's in the Easy Rider movie. And then we rode over to Canon City to see Buskskin Joe's. Now it was time to head back on the road again, so we took off back to Colorado Springs and dropped off Cuzzin Paul's and my Cuzzin Peggy at her place.

Then Cuzzin Paul on his Honda 550 wanted to go ride over Independence Pass, which was about 2 hours kinda west of us,…so we did. Beautiful country, for sure. Elevation there at the summit is a bit over 12,000 feet, so the 3 Hondas were having some "issues" once again with the thin air, but they did better this time than they did going up Pikes Peak, which is even 2,000 feet higher. On this segment of the trip, we rode through the then-brand-new Eisenhower Tunnel, which is 1.8 miles long, the longest and highest tunnel I have ever ridden in my 49 years of Two Wheeled Life, and the trusty ol' 67 Ironhead sounded really good in there. Few things are more fun than listening to your pipes in a really loooooong tunnel, right?

From Independence Pass to Denver is about another 2 hours. And here is one funny thing that happened on that segment of the trip. The 67 Sportster and the 3 Hondas all got filled with gas next to Independence Pass, then we took off toward Denver and when we got about half way, the 3 Honda guys were wanting to pull over for gas again, so we rode into a gas station.

When I pulled the gas cap off the Sportster's big turtle tank, I looked inside and I could still touch the gas, it hadn't used much at all. Hmm. So, they filled their tanks and we hit the road again. Went maybe another hour or so and they wanted to get gas again. This time I decided to put some gas in the Sportster, and it held exactly 1.0 gallons of gas, and on the odometer it said we had gone 72 miles since its last fill up. Yep, that Sportster got 72 miles on one gallon of gas, and I have had people tell me that is bullshit before, but it was true. Granted, you are going downhill from Independence Pass toward Denver, but I'm tellin' ya, up in that high Colorado elevation the Tillotson carb performed flawlessly and that ol' Ironhead motor ran as smooth as glass. Once we got passed Denver, things got a little messed up. The 2 brothers on the Honda 350s were wearing out and could no longer keep up the pace. They were sayin' that their butts hurt and they were talking about going back to Fort Worth.

I looked at Cuzzin Paul, and I was hoping his 2 friends would go back to Fort Worth, not because I was rude, but because I only had 14 days to do this entire trip, and the days were already slipping away and we were nowhere close to the Canadian Border yet,…see?

But they were his friends he had known since they were kids, and I was the young whippersnapper on the trip, so I kinda kept my mouth shut and let Paul and his 2 buddies hash it out. I mean, even if Paul wanted to ditch the trip and go back home with them, I understood. But I had "A Goal" to meet, and that goal was the Canadian Border, and if I did not make it, I would catch hell from all my friends back in Dallas that said I would never make it there in the first place, bwahahaha. So the bet was on. The deal was I had to mail some friends post cards from Calgary to prove I made it. When I got back to Dallas that would mean free beer for me, and who doesn't like free beer? And yes, I know I was only 18 years old at this time but back then 18-year-olds could legally get into bars, if ya remember?

If Cuzzin Paul wanted to ride back to DFW with his buddies, I understood, and I was certainly prepared to ride on alone because that was my original plan in the first place. This was supposed to be my "Then Came Bronson" solo trip anyhow. Paul and his 2 buddies came into the picture later. Well, after the three of them had 'The Talk', the 2 brothers decided to ride back to Fort Worth and Cuzzin Paul wanted to stick to the Canadian Border Plan.

So we parted ways on the north side of Denver. The two brothers took off headed back to Fort Worth, and I have never meant any disrespect to them for turning back. After all, they were on Honda 350s, and whoever heard of taking a little bike like that out on a long road trip? I mean, those two guys can honestly tell everyone that they rode their Honda 350s from Fort Worth to the summit of Pikes Peak and back, and I will vouch for them, I got respect for them for doing that. But meanwhile, back on the road, I told Paul I was running out of time and said we needed to make up some good time and get into Wyoming, if possible, that very night. It was already gettin' pretty dark. Paul was a trooper and agreed, so off we rode, headed into the evening hours, next stop Wyoming.

We finally hit the Wyoming Border pretty late at night. Here is the photo from that dark moment in time, hah. That's me on the 67 Sportster at the bottom of the Wyoming sign and you can barely see the orange tent packed on the back,…kinda. Now,…where in the hell will we sleep?

1973 Cross Country Trip from Dallas to Canada

Part 6

Last semi exciting chapter we left off with the group of 4 bikes getting whittled down to just 2 bikes, my Cuzzin Paul on his nice new Honda 550 and me on the 67 Sportster. The 2 brothers had turned back to Fort Worth after successfully riding up to Pikes Peak Summit. So Paul and I headed on toward Wyoming, on the way to Canada, the final destination. Paul and I rode into the Wyoming border around midnight I'd guess, cuz the sky was pitch black there at the border sign.

And speaking of how dark it was, we were from Dallas and were used to having bright city lights around and not being able to see very many stars at night. But out here on the border of Wyoming at night with the pitch-black sky, there seemed to be millions of stars up in the sky and everything was still and quiet, except for an occasional 18-wheeler that went whizzing by us while we were taking the picture in the dark at the Wyoming border sign.

But so much for looking at the stars, we gotta get going again and find some semi decent place to crash for a few hours. In Colorado, I had mentioned to Paul to forget the tents that night, let's keep riding and get in some miles and find a cheapie motel to crash at for a few hours rest, and he said OK. So we pushed on to Cheyenne, thinking we'd find plenty of motel rooms in that medium size town. But we were dead wrong.

When we first rode into the south side of Cheyenne, which is waaaay down in the bottom south east corner of the state, all the motel parking lots were full,…like,…so full it was eerie.

Every motel and hotel had up a No Vacancy sign. What the fuck is going on now? We finally pulled into one of the bigger motels, probably either a Howard Johnson or Holiday Inn, I forget, but it had tons of rooms there, but they were all full up, No Vacancy. And when we walked in, the guy at the desk told us there was no way we were gonna find a motel room anywhere around for a distance of 50 miles or more, cuz there was a frickin' cattle buyers' convention in town. We were totally fucked! No place to sleep,…for miles in any direction.

So we filled our gas tanks in the dark at a gas station, pondering what to do next? We kinda idled around town until we saw a high school with an overhead roof at the main entrance, like a roof to keep the snow or rain off the kids during winter time. And the high school entrance was kinda hidden in the dark, no bright lights shinin' on it, so we pulled both our bikes in to the front porch of that high school, shut them off, turned off our lights, and threw our sleeping bags down on the concrete sidewalk and went to sleep on the concrete with the crickets chirping so loud it was crazy. Try that sometime, hahaha.

Of course we woke up really early the next morning cuz it was probably already pretty close to morning when we went to sleep,… right? We found a little cafe, had a nice breakfast, then our sore butts went back out to the bikes and started off again. And we're ridin' north on I-25 headed through Casper on to Sheridan and then into Montana, Big Sky Country, which was about 350 miles away. And then we still had quite a few miles after that to get to the Canadian Border. Damn it all, will we ever get there?

This picture here is one Cuzzin Paul took while we were hauling ass down the road in northern Wyoming, and that is my brand- new buckskin fringe jacket I had just gotten at the base of Pikes Peak in Manitou Springs. And I could kick back on this 67 Sportster and relax cuz it had The Original Cruise Control, the 'dangerous' throttle that never snapped back, and that throttle soon got outlawed, along with the Sportster's classy right side foot shift.

THE EARLY YEARS

1973 Cross Country Trip from Dallas to Canada

Part 7

We left off last time sleeping on the front porch of the Cheyenne high school cuz there was a cattle buyers' convention in town and no motel rooms for us road weary riders, sigh. Was it fun tryin' to sleep on fuckin' concrete? Sure, why not, hah. It was sooo much fun that I can still laugh about it these 49 years later, wink, wink. But hey, at least the cattle buyers got nice comfy motel rooms, eh?

So, we dragged ourselves off the hard concrete and packed the stuff back on the two bikes. We found a place to eat breakfast and gassed up the bikes and took off from there and continued on up I-90 North through Sheridan toward Montana. It was a ride of maybe 350 miles or so. Anyhow, we finally made it to the Big Sky Border and here I am wearing the new buckskin fringe jacket at the Montana border sign.

I offered to take Cuzzin Paul's picture at stops along the way, but I think he mighta been afraid that I'd drop or maybe ruin his expensive camera, who knows? So, you gotta look at my mug most of the time lucky you, wink, wink. Next stop? Custer's Last Stand at Little Big Horn.

THE EARLY YEARS

1973 Cross Country Trip from Dallas to Canada

Part 8

We left off last time finally riding into Montana. And riding north up I-90/I-25 or whatever they call it today, from Cheyenne Wyoming to Little Big Horn in Crow Agency is about 400 miles and that's where we found ourselves next. It was a good day's ride. Ya gotta remember, this was 1973 and the speed limit was 55 back then, so averaging 50 mph and 400 miles a day was a decent day's work, I mean "fun" for us, ha ha- ha.

We got off the bikes at Little Big Horn and walked around the site where Custer met his Waterloo. According to what we read on the markers back then, they originally buried the guys right where they fell, then later moved their remains to a group grave, I think?

Anyhow, here's the pictures from Little Big Horn. You can see how the battle went and where they fell. And we got a photo of Custer and another one of his leather fringe field uniforms in a glass case. I was a-lookin' for some arrow holes in it but I never saw any. My new Pikes Peak fringe got to meet Custer's old Little Big Horn fringe. We camped out this night not too far away from Little Big Horn. Didn't see, hear, or smell any ghosts all night long.

THE EARLY YEARS

1973 Cross Country Trip from Dallas to Canada

Part 9

We left off in our last semi-thrilling episode with the 67 Sportster and the Honda 550 being at Custer's Little Big Horn battlefield up in Crow Agency, Montana. We still got a ways to get our sore butts to the Canadian Border. It was still roughly 500 miles from Billings to Calgary and we were not making very good time. I don't mean to whine, but here goes, hahaha.

Cuzzin Paul, bless his pea-pickin' heart, was lucky he had some nice vacation time, so he was in no big hurry on this trip. Time meant nothing to him. He was a 21 year old college student studying to be an architect, and he was out of school for the entire summer. He could be a motorsickle bum and do whatever he wanted. He was free.

On the other hand, I was an 18 year old punk kid fresh outta high school and I had gotten accepted into the Dallas Carpenter Apprentice School, and I had a job waiting for me that started in 2 weeks. I was to begin working on the Braniff Terminal at the DFW International Airport, which was to be the largest airport in the world at that time, still under construction.

So I had to get to Canada and get back home, kinda fast. And this trip was originally to be a solo run I was doing, in the "Then Came Bronson" old Sportster style, and then Paul joined at the next to the last minute. But I am glad he rode along, cuz we did have a blast and I would not have these pictures if he had not gone. So I will stop whining now.

THE EARLY YEARS

OK well I am gonna whine a little bit more, I was expecting us to ride together kinda like Captain America and Billy did in Easy Rider, side by side most of the time. But that seldom, if ever, happened. Cuzzin Paul would be there beside me, then suddenly he would be in gones-ville. Maybe he was 100 yards behind me? Or maybe he would be 300 yards behind me? Or maybe he would be a 1/4 mile back behind me? Or maybe he would be totally out of sight, hahaha?

I don't know how many times I would pull over on the side of the road and wait for him to catch up. A coupla times I'd pull over and wait on the idling Sportster and still not see him, so I would do a Bat Turn in the middle of the road and go riding back looking for him, wondering if he had broken down, ya know? Maybe I'd ride back a half mile or so, and there he would be, sitting on the side of the road. I'd ask him "What's up?" He'd point out in the distance and say stuff like "Look at that hawk out there" or "isn't that a fantastic cloud formation?"

OK, that's a nice hawk and all is fine and dandy with the clouds, but we ain't gettin' any miles in, hahaha. In the beginning when I was mapping out this road trip, I had allowed 4 days to get to Calgary, 4 days to spend ridin' around in Canada, then 4 days to ride back to Dallas. That = 12 days on the road and just over 4,000 miles,…see? I had to be back in Dallas in order to go to work on a brand new job. And I had a grand total of 14 days, so if I had a breakdown or any really bad weather, I still had a 2 day cushion.

But the deal is, we spent the first night camping at Palo Duro Canyon at the KOA Kampground, still in Texas, the second night with sleeping bags on the living room floor at Cuzzin Peggy's apartment in Colorado Springs, and the third night still at Cuzzin Peggy's place, and the fourth night was sleeping on the front porch of the high school in Cheyenne, Wyoming, and the fifth night was camping outside Crow Agency, Montana, by Little Big Horn. And here we were, our sixth day out on the road, and we ain't even out of Montana yet? Bummer, dude.

At Billings we cut up kinda straight north on the little red state highways in my pocket size Road Atlas that I still have today and those little highways changed numbers a few times so I don't remember what they were, but they were headed to the Canadian border in the straightest line possible. Then came the Canadian Border,... finally.

Now Cuzzin Paul and I had been raised in Dallas, Texas, and we were kinda used to Big City Lights & Sights. And we were both thinking the Canadian Border would be a destination of sorts, like lights, action, bars, booze, restaurants, diners, truck stops, shit like that. Boy howdy were we wrong.

When we got to the border, it was a lonely dinky little road going down to kinda nowhere, with this thing like a school crossing guard's shack for the border guards to get bored and hang out in, So here it is, finally,...the Magnificent and Glorious Canadian Border! We finally made it. Behold!

1973 Cross Country Trip from Dallas to Canada

Part 10

We were just arriving to the Canadian Border,…a dinky little road kinda out in the middle of nowhere up north on the Montana border.

When I was a 'Then Came Bronson' and 'Easy Rider' freak in high school, everybody told me I would never get a Sportster and never ride it cross country, let alone all the way to Canada. They said that was fake shit for TV shows. They called it a Pipe Dream.

So then the friends and family said shit like "Well, OK, so you got the Sportster, big deal. Just because you got it doesn't mean you can actually ride it across country for long distances."

I told them I was gonna ride that thing all the way up to Canada. They said "you will never make it all the way to Canada from here in Dallas. That is too far to ride on a motorcycle. You are crazy and just plain fulla bullshit."

Of course, all that whinin' shit just made me wanna do it even worse. So here's to all those naysayer folks who said 18 year old me would never make it all the way to Canada on an old used Sportster. Touché. And this is the picture Cuzzin Paul took of his Honda there at the border sign with the 67 Ironhead and me.

SHOVELHEAD DAVE

1973 Cross Country Trip from Dallas to Canada

Part 11

So, we were at the Canadian Border, kinda out in the middle of nowhere. It was all fine and dandy that we made it to the border, but the goal was Calgary, Alberta. Why Calgary? I dunno, hahaha.

Well, maybe I do. Ya see in high school I was a rodeo cowboy, rode bulls, did chute doggin' and did the wild mare race. There was a Canadian bull rider guy that hung out at The Kow Bell Rodeo Arena in Mansfield, Texas, west of Fort Worth a bit.

Anyhow, the guy's name was Sandy and he always blabbed about Calgary, like it was The Place to be, and they had the Calgary Stampede Rodeo, shit like that. So it made me kinda curious as to what it was like.

Now, couple that wanderlust thinking with 'Then Came Bronson' and 'Easy Rider' and you can kinda see where this idea was formed…right?

Calgary was maybe a 2-to-3-hour ride away from the border, so off we went, in search of Calgary. The first town of any size that we ran into along the way was Lethbridge. We made it to there, ate and got gas, and Cuzzin Paul took this picture out at the edge of town.

SHOVELHEAD DAVE

1973 Cross Country Trip from Dallas to Canada

Part 12

We left off last time riding into Lethbridge, Alberta. We ate and got gas, then hit the road again. We had about 2- and 1/2-hours ride to get to Calgary. It was a really nice putt through the countryside with really good weather, like heaven, and of course no traffic. At times it seemed like we were the only ones on the road.

Riding from Lethbridge toward Calgary, we rode up over the crest of a hill and I will never forget the sight that pounced on us. Picture a beautiful blue sky above you, a nice fresh two lane blacktop ribbon road you are ridin' on, and then everything around you as far as you can see is the brightest yellow you can imagine. It was like looking at a giant yellow ocean with its waves blowing in the wind, for as many miles as we could see, to our left and to our right. Just blue sky above us, yellow ground all around us with a little black road windin' through the middle of it. If your mind is working like mine, you might be having a flashback to the Wizard of Oz movie when the travelers get into the giant yellow field of poppies, hah. But these weren't poppies. Later when we pulled into a gas station, I asked the guy what all that yellow was. He said it was flax plants. So that solves the Big Yellow Mystery.

When we got into Calgary, we just rode around downtown some to check it out. We stayed there for the night and got a cheapie motel room, washed clothes and slept on real beds for a change. Hell we even had a steak dinner and some nice booze to celebrate getting there.

This is a photo Cuzzin Paul took of Calgary, which was a bit smaller city back in 1973, eh?

SHOVELHEAD DAVE

1973 Cross Country Trip from Dallas to Canada

Part 13

We finally got to ride into Calgary in the last segment of this semi boring 1967 Sportster tale, so we made it to the destination… big yay. Back in Palo Duro Canyon I had my doubts we'd make it.

So we got steak dinners and Canadian beers that night, paid for it with multi colored Canadian money, got to sleep on real beds and even got to wash our clothes and start all over again the next day,… and we took showers even,…gasp.

Cuzzin Paul wanted to hit the Honda shop so we did and he got a Calgary Honda t shirt and some motor oil for his change, then we rode over to the Calgary Harley shop and I got a t shirt, 4 quarts of oil for a change, and for some reason still unknown to me,… I got a stuffed AMF Harley Davidson Penguin. Don't ask me why, though.

Maybe I thought we were close to the North Pole so I wanted the Penguin to show I nearly made it to the North Pole? Maybe it was because I was still an 18-year-old snot nosed punk kid and thought Penguins lived at the North Pole when they don't, cuz they live at the South Pole? I dunno. All I know is I got the AMF Penguin, had to pack it with me the rest of the trip and yes, I still have it out in the garage over the workbench. It is now 49 years old. Never throw anything good away?

Next up on the agenda was riding over to Banff, cuz everybody we talked to in Calgary told us we should go see that town.

Banff sits right in the middle of the mountains like it is in Switzerland, or so they said. So we took off for there. Why not, right? It was only an hour and a half ride away, so they said, and it was over on the far western side of the Province of Alberta. And one thing I should mention about the Canadians, they were some of the nicest and friendliest people I have ever encountered.

Maybe it was because we were riding motorsickles and they felt sorry for us or thought we were crazy? All I know is our two white and black Texas license tags sure stood out there and attracted attention at the gas stations, campgrounds, bars and cafes we went to.

After gassing up the bikes, off we rode to Banff, on a beautiful winding road through the nice countryside. One thing I liked about riding in Canada was their road signs for their highways, they had signs with the maple leaf on them and we were on Maple Leaf #1, headed to Banff. And the towns we rode through had kinda funny names, Morley, Ozada, Kananaskis- (try saying that one 3 times fast)- and then my favorite one was called Dead Man's Flats, then Canmore, and finally Mount Rundle and then into Banff, which has an elevation of around 4,500 feet. So now we were in the Canadian Rockies, with their Cascade Mountain, with an elevation of 9,836 feet.

This photo is on the road kinda outside Calgary before we got into the higher country near Banff.

1973 Cross Country Trip from Dallas to Canada

Part 14

Our last stop we had the bikes packed up, leaving Calgary headed for Banff, Alberta. That means we were gonna be headed back into semi-high elevation where the new Honda 550 with 4 cylinders might have some more thin air issues but the ol' 67 Sportster still ran just fine. The elevation at Banff is around 4,500 feet, so it wasn't like we were headed up to 14,000 feet like Pikes Peak again, at least. And Banff has to be one of the most beautiful places I have ever seen, anywhere I have ever ridden. We left taking their Maple Leaf Highway 1 sign out of Calgary and headed straight into the Rocky Mountains. The weather was fantastic, the air was clear, it was like riding in a joint even better than heaven.

I remember that one place along the way called Dead Man's Flats. I hoped we didn't end up that way riding off the side of some mountain pass, I mean, you could ride off one of those passes on the side of the road and head straight down hundreds of feet to rocks and trees, and maybe even a river at the bottom, and if no one in a car saw you go over the edge, it might be years before anyone found your carcass…after the bears ate you, right, ha ha ha? It's not like we had cell phones to call back then in 1973. Sliding off the side of the road would be some scary business, for sure.

Another thing I had fun with on this trip that made a good memory was their Canadian money. Their 1-, 5, 10 and 20- dollar bills were all different colors. It was exciting pulling out a wad of different colored bills just to get 2 bucks worth of gas at some mountain station, at least for this 18-year-old punk kid it was. But then again, maybe I am easily amused?

We eventually got into Banff and all the stories we had heard about how beautiful it is, turned out to be true. Banff has big rugged mountains sticking straight up out of the ground up to the sky, right at the edge of town.

Banff is also one of their National Parks, so there is plenty of camping everywhere and we got a really nice camping spot and threw up the tents and started a camp fire that evening. And in the winter time, I could see how Banff would be all covered in tons of snow, and they said they have lots of snow skiing action there in the winter time. But I ain't into winter time snow skiing, I am into summer time motorsicklin'. Here is a picture Cuzzin Paul took of the Main Drag in Banff, looking up the end of the street.

1973 Cross Country Trip from Dallas to Canada

Part 15

Last time we left off camping for the night in Banff, Alberta. The next day, we thought since we were already on the far western side of Alberta, we might as well ride over the border and go into British Columbia. That way we could say we rode in two different Canadian Provinces…right?

So after we broke camp, we had a nice breakfast at a little cafe and then gassed up the motorsickles and headed on over to British Columbia. We were just riding around taking in the scenery. This beautiful lush mountain scenery in BC was a far cry from the flat dusty landscape we were both used to in Texas.

We were not interested in making any road time just yet, still just puttin' around having fun. But soon, we would hafta be back on the interstates hauling ass, mainly in order for me to get back to Dallas to start that new job building the DFW Airport.

Cuzzin Paul was still on his summer vacation for several more weeks, in this picture we are on the side of the road in Alberta next to the BC Border, and we are trying to figure out which highway we wanna take next. Decisions, decisions. Imagine having the biggest worry of your day to be deciding which beautiful mountain highway is best to ride your Ironhead Sportster on that day?

SHOVELHEAD DAVE

1973 CROSS COUNTRY TRIP FROM DALLAS TO CANADA

Part 16

Here's another photo of the beautiful mountainous area in western Alberta and eastern British Columbia around Banff where we were riding and camping back in 1973. Wonder if it's all condos now?

Camping out here was some of the most peaceful camping I have ever done, and I spent quite a few years riding cross country and camping out. Banff National Park in Alberta has the Bow River twisting through its mountains, plus a few pristine lakes which are certainly frozen over in the winter time. I'd hate to be riding there in the winter time though. The Banff area has to be one of the most beautiful places on the North American continent.

I feel very lucky to have been riding an old used 1967 Sportster through all that rugged territory back then. I had three friends in high school who swore they would also get bikes and we'd take off cross country on a group ride. But,…not one of them ever got a bike. Too bad for them. Look at this trip they missed out on. What were they doing at this time, anyhow? Hangin' out at a Sonic Drive-In, gnawin' on some greasy burgers while I am riding and camping up here in beautiful Banff? Probably. They told me I'd never make it this far. Well, I did.

Camping at night in this area was a lot of fun. Big black wide-open sky over our heads, fulla stars, the sound of crystal-clear water running over the rocks in the river next to us, our little campfire going while we sat there and drank Moosehead Beers. We were just trying to soak it all in. Enjoy this while it lasts, cuz it will soon be over. sigh. And we weren't putting in all that many miles at this stage of the trip. We were just kinda casually riding through this strange prehistoric looking land which was new to us two Dallas boys. And we had to save our butts right now, cuz soon we were gonna hafta ride the 2,000 miles back to Dallas. Now I am not 100% sure about this photo, cuz I never lived there and don't remember seeing any signs, but I think this is the 9,800-foot-high Cascade Mountain in Banff National Park.

1973 Cross Country Trip from Dallas to Canada

Part 17

Last time we left off just puttin' around in Alberta and BC, camping out and enjoying the scenic mountainous countryside.

It was fun having our pockets full of colorful Canadian money and looking at the Dodge trucks that said "FARGO" on their tailgates. And the Imperial gallons of gas were fun, although they seemed to cost quite a bit more. After all, this trip was during the first gas shortage when the national speed limit was reduced to 55 mph. Remember when they were telling us we were running outta gas? One older guy I knew in Dallas said we started running outta gas the instant the first oil well was drilled. Maybe he was right?

Anyhow, back up here in the Canadian mountains, the rivers were so crystal clear you could see the rocks and pebbles on the bottoms of the rivers, even if they were 15 or 20 feet deep. The air was fresh, the people were nice. The trees were high. It was heaven on earth.

But soon all of that was gonna come to an end, cuz it would be time for us to head back on the highway to Dallas. But before we pack up the 67 Sportster and the 4 Cylinder Honda for the 2,000-mile ride back, here is one last photo Cuzzin Paul took of the area where we had been riding for the past few days. We were riding on that road below in the photo and it snaked its way back up here on top. So, Paul pulled over and pointed down and said 'that's where we were.' Then he snapped this picture. And next it's gonna be time to head back to Dallas, which is around 2,000 miles away, Gulp.

SHOVELHEAD DAVE

1973 Cross Country Trip from Dallas to Canada

Part 18

"The Strange Ending of the Trip"

To recap, this 1973 Cross Country Road Trip started out with 4 of us, 3 were on new Hondas, 21-year-old Cuzzin Paul on his 4 cylinder 550 and the other 2 friends of his that were riding 350s, and then 18-year-old me on my 6-year-old 67 Sportster.

Our first night on the road we camped at Palo Duro Canyon in the Texas Panhandle. Second night we threw sleeping bags on the floor at our Cuzzin Peggy's apartment in Colorado Springs and we rode up Pikes Peak, rode across the Royal Gorge Bridge and went to Buckskin Joe's. Third night was still sleeping at Peggy's place.

By the fourth night, it was just Cuzzin Paul and me since the two 350s decided to head back to Dallas, and that fourth night we slept on the concrete front porch of the high school in Cheyenne, Wyoming, due to the cattle buyers' convention in town hoggin' up all the motel rooms for a 50-mile radius, so they told us.

Fifth night we camped out by Custer's Last Stand at Little Big Horn in Montana. Sixth night we got a motel room in Calgary, Alberta and had been camping in the mountains around Banff and into the edge of British Columbia the past 3 nights.

So now this is Day 10 of the 1973 Cross Country Road Trip, and it is time to for me to get my saddle-sore butt back to Dallas, which we were thinking would be a 4 day ride, around 2,000 miles to go. Not only did I have to be there to start a new job, I had to be there to get enrolled in the Dallas Carpenter Apprentice School, so there were no ifs, ands, or buts about it. I HAD to be there on time. We rolled up our tents and sleeping bags, packed the two bikes, and headed off to whatever diner we could find up the highway for breakfast and gas for the bikes.

We had been up by Golden British Columbia where their Glacier National Park is, and the road south we were planning on taking was Highway 95, which became Highway 93 once it got into Montana. Kalispell was the first town of any size we recognized on my little Road Atlas pocket book map, so that's where we decided we were headed. Paul always carried his camera and I always had the map in my fringe jacket pocket, that was the deal.

At the little road side joint where we ate breakfast, we changed what was left of our colorful Canadian paper money back into boring USA greenbacks, filled our gas tanks with the last Imperial Gallons, and headed south back toward homes-ville, aka Dallas, Texas. For those of you who have been paying semi- close attention to this rambling of the road trip, you might remember how it seemed to me that Cuzzin Paul had a funny riding style, as in riding next to me, then suddenly 50 feet behind me, then maybe 300 yards back, then 1/4 mile back, then suddenly out of sight.

Sometimes I would pull the Sportster over onto the side of the road and sit there idling, waiting for him to catch up, while a few other times I had to turn around and go riding back down the road looking for him. And in the back of my mind, I always had a semi-uneasy feeling that he may have slid off the side of the road or maybe a car ran him off the road or perhaps a deer hit him or a giant rock fell out of the cliff above us, who knows? Anything can happen out there in the wide-open wilderness.

It sorta bugged me when he was not riding side by side. But, different strokes for different folks. Looking back, maybe the Sportster's pipes were too loud for him and he didn't like being that close,… who knows? Anyhow, as we were riding south down the road toward the Canada/US border, suddenly Paul was gone again. I pulled over and waited, but he never showed. I turned the Sportster back up the road from where it had come from and I rode back looking for Paul.

I searched the area where I had last seen him, but never found him. I rode really slow over the areas where there were no guard rails, wondering if my Cuzzin was down there on the jagged rocks somewhere. I never saw him. I did not know what to do. It was as if a UFO had beamed Paul up to outer space. He was just,…gone. And to you younger folks who may be reading this, no, there was no such thing as a cell phone, ha ha ha.

Against my feeling for leaving a family member, I finally made the tough decision to head for the Canada/Montana Border as we originally planned, cuz I figured that's what Paul knew and would probably do. Maybe he turned off on some little side road that I didn't even see? Who knows? My thinking was maybe he took a wrong turn but we would eventually hook up at the border again.

So I got to the Canadian Border by myself. Now riding into Canada was no big deal. The Canadian guards just looked at us, asked where we were from, asked where we were headed and if we had enough money to make it, then they let us through. No big deal at all. But riding back into the USA was a totally different story. The USA guards made me strip everything off the Sportster and they went through my fringe jacket, the orange nylon tent and its bag, my sleeping bag, the duffel bag with clothes, my bike tools and they made me empty the pockets in my jeans. They even looked suspiciously at the stuffed AMF Penguin I had picked up at the Calgary H-D Dealer. They ran me through the wringer like I was an escaped convict on the run. But… I made it through.

While all of that intense inspection was going on at the border, I asked the guards if they had seen my Cuzzin Paul on his Honda 550 all packed up with road gear and a white and black Texas license tag on it. They said no, so that made me think he had not been through the border yet. So, I waited a coupla hours for Paul at the border. He never showed.

I made the operator-assisted long distance phone call to my folks back in Dallas to let them know what was up. Paul's mom was my dad's younger sister, that was our related connection, and I asked my folks to call his folks and let them know what was going on. Next, I decided to head on to Kalispell, Montana, since Paul knew that's where we were headed…right?

After I made it through the border, I headed on down the road and got a campsite at a campground there and phoned my folks back in Dallas again and told them where I was now. I asked them if Paul's folks had heard from him. It was a 4-way phone tag through long distance pay phones. And for you young-uns that may be unaware, a pay phone was usually in a thing called a 'phone booth' and you might find them at gas stations, cafes, drug stores, grocery stores, bus stations, or maybe in campgrounds, and you had to put coins in it to make it work and they had dials on them. And in the middle of your conversation, an operator would butt in and tell you to add more money or she would cut you off. That's the way it was back then.

I had an uneasy sleep that night worried about Cuzzin Paul. The next morning, I broke camp, packed the road gear on the Sportster, ate breakfast, and called my folks back home again. They had heard from Paul's folks and his folks had told my folks that he was still in Canada, ha-ha. I guess he was taking it easy all that time. Anyhow, I had to get back to Dallas, muy pronto, cuz I had that new carpenter apprentice job waiting to start at the DFW Airport, working on the brand new Braniff Terminal which was being built.

From Kalispell to Dallas was around 1,800 miles I had to cover. So I kicked over that ol' Red 67 Sportster and it and me finally had my high school dream going, of being my very own version of "Then Came Bronson." It actually felt kinda weird riding alone now, just the Red 67 Sportster and me. We rode through magnificent country, under clear wide-open skies, over the mountains, across the rivers and lakes and across the plains we ventured. Just it and me,…just like Jim Bronson, at last.

I had endless ribbons of wide-open highway in front of me and the 900 cc Sportster exhaust note behind me. I never got tired of listening to the Sportster's solid lifter motor or its exhaust pipes. I loved them both. All the last 4 years I had spent in school, 1969 to 1973, sitting at a boring school desk wanting to be out on the open road all by myself like Bronson finally came true,…by accident.

I rode through Montana, then Wyoming, then into Colorado where something horrible happened. I was riding along in Colorful Colorado when suddenly it felt like my left arm caught on fire, like a lightning bolt hit it. I was like,…what the fuck? It was burning like hell and almost made me wipe out. I was reaching across my chest with my right hand grabbing and squeezing my left arm which started out hurting at my wrist, then went up my forearm to my elbow and then on up to my shoulder. What the fuck is this, a heart attack on an 18-year- old kid out in the middle of Colorado?

I pulled the Sportster over onto the shoulder of the highway and shut it off and yanked off that buckskin fringe jacket. Then down there at my feet was a big ol' crumpled up pissed off hornet, and that fucker had blown up the sleeve of the jacket and had been stinging me multiple times going up my arm. A bee can only sting you once and then its stinger falls out and it dies, but a hornet can sting you 10 or 15 times just for the hell of it and that's what I now had going on. I stomped that fucking hornet into oblivion, its guts were spread out on the gravel on the side of that highway and its worries were now over.

But my arm was now throbbing to beat the band and swelling up and turning red. I got back on the Sportster and headed on down the highway and the next little mom & pop gas station/general store that came up, I pulled over and went inside and got some Baking Soda from the little lady and made up a paste of that and water to put on my left arm. My mom had taught me that Baking Soda trick when I was younger, but she never said anything about the six pack of cold frosty Coors I also got to drink while I sat under their tree at the gas station waiting for the throbbing to subside. The Coors was my own invention for pain relief.

OK so in the grand scheme of things, those hornet stings were just a minor diversion and I still had many miles to go. I headed on to New Mexico until I got back onto familiar turf in Texas. I made the 1,800 miles in 3 days. I ain't got one single picture of the trip back cuz I didn't have a camera. You will just hafta take my word that I made it back,…alive.

Paul also made it back to Dallas safe and sound, 2 days after I got there, so it was a happy ending after all for everybody. A coupla weeks later, Paul gave me these wonderful pictures of our awesome road trip, which I will cherish til I'm dead. Oh,…and the Braniff International Terminal got built.

This photo here is the last one Paul took of me, and there I am, intentionally violating the Canadian Helmet Law. Gasp! Paul and me were talking about being forced to wear helmets and how we were getting tired of wearing them day after day after day after day. Paul sez to me, "Why don't you pull your helmet off and go back down the road, then ride this way and I'll take a picture of you with no helmet on, breakin' the helmet law?" So I did.

1973 Cross Country Trip from Dallas to Canada

PS: Extra Part 19 "Souvenirs"

I am not the current owner of the old Red 1967 Sportster that took me on this fun road trip to Canada. I rode it for one year after the trip and then sold it to my high school buddy Freddie in order to get the 1974 Shovelhead in July of 1974 that I still ride today. The 67 Sportster is probably still out there somewhere and I'm guessing the current owner has no idea what that old motorsickle did back in 1973. That trusty ol' 1967 Sportster was what I cut my 'Sickle Road Trip Teeth on and I will always be an Ironhead Sportster fan down to my bone marrow. I'd still be riding it if I wasn't 6 foot 4 and needed more room on a bike.

I'm glad I had the old photos to share with you folks from the 1973 Canada Road Trip. And while I don't have any pictures of the solo ride back, I do have some pictures I took recently of the 3 souvenirs I got from that 1973 Canada trip.

Here's that ol' 1973 Pikes Peak buckskin fringe jacket I still have, and here's the AMF Penguin from the Calgary H-D Dealer and my Official Calgary Stampede Silver Dollar, even though it ain't made out of real silver. And they are on the 74 AMF Shovel Chopper I've been ridin' since 1974.

SHOVELHEAD DAVE

"Whatever Happened to the 1973 Canada Road Trip '67 Sportster?"

In the spring of 1974, I sold the 67 Sportster to my pal Freddie in order to get the 74 Super Glide on July 11, 1974, during the middle of the AMF Strike. Freddie and I rode together on these 2 bikes from 1974 until 1976. We rode down to Galveston, Padre Island, Texarkana, Springtown, Azle, all Texas trips.

Then in 1976 Freddie got married and his new missus put an end to him ridin' a dangerous motorsickle, oh my, so I bought it back from him and I kept it until late 1977 when I sold it to another friend named Alan.

Alan got a loan from the bank for it, and then got behind in payments and the bank re-po'ed it.

Next thing I know, I'm in Mid Cities HD Dealer in Arlington, Texas, and there sits this very same 67 Sportster XLH, cuz they had just bought it at the bank auction. Wealthy Dude Gene was originally from California and now he was the new owner of the HD dealership which had previously been Ivey's Harley Davidson where I got the 74. See how all this ties together?

Joe Cox was Gene's head mechanic at the dealership who would later build my second stroker motor for me in the winter of 1979. Anyhow, I was standing there that day in 1977 looking at my old friend, the 67 Sportster, and Gene came up to me and asked me if I wanted to buy it, I told him I had already bought that bike,…twice. Told him I rode it to Canada in 1973, then bought it again in 1976. Then I told Gene how I still had all the original XLH dresser parts for it, the big white buddy seat, the leg crash bar, windshield, and the white fiberglass saddlebags.

Gene got kinda excited and asked me on the spot if I wanted to sell those parts to him. I looked at Joe who was standing there and I said to Gene, "Uh,…yeah. I'll sell those parts to you for uh,…500 bucks." Gene nearly shit. (My house payment was $104 back then, hahaha.) Gene sez "500 bucks is crazy money for those parts. There is no way those parts are worth that much money." I said "Now you know what all your customers feel like buying parts from you."

Gene walked away and I kept the parts. A few months later, Gene decided to sell the Red 67 Sportster to Joe Cox. And when I found out Joe was now the owner, I gave him all the parts for free, just to piss Gene off some more. And the last time I saw this fine trusty Sportster, it still belonged to Joe Cox and he had put it all back to stock with the bags and windshield returning it to its roots. That was in 1979.

Spring of 1980 I packed the sleeping bag and tent on the 74 Shovel Chopper and left Texas to go live in the mountains in Washington State, and I never saw the 67 Sportster again.

Here are 3 old photos for you. One where Freddie just got it from me, one with my new love, the 74 Shovel in front of it, and the last picture is in front of my house in Dallas from 1976 when I got the Sportster back from Freddie. Notice he had it repainted and some chrome work done on the motor. Wonder where it is today? And no, I do not remember the VIN number, rats.

So now that I had a bike of my own again, that meant Freddie and me could start taking some little trips on the two Harleys. And I'm tellin' ya, it was kinda tough watching Freddie havin' fun ridin' around on the ol' familiar 67 Sportster while I was stuck with just a car for wheels.

But now them days are over and I will never be without a motor-sickle again. Ever. And that is one promise I made to myself back then that I have kept ever since,…to never again be without a bike. And now that the 74 AMF Super Glide was a brand new bike, it needed to be broken in kinda carefully,…according to the dealer. That meant Freddie and me rode mostly in the Dallas-Fort Worth area at first. And since it was hot Texas summer time, whenever we'd be ridin' out by Lake Dallas or Possum Kingdom out west of Fort Worth, and since we were 19 year olds, that meant we'd park the bikes by the lake and go jump in to cool off. And no,…we were not skinny dippin' cuz there wuz families around, didn't wanna shock the little kids. We'd jump in with our clothes on and it didn't matter, cuz once we got back on the bikes and started ridin', we'd be dried off in no time flat.

And then came the Maiden Voyage Time for the 74 Super Glide. In the summertime, a lotta Texas teenagers head down to Galveston. So that's what we decided to do for our first semi- long virgin run. Galveston is roughly 300 miles from Dallas so that would be a decent distance run to get the Super Glide's feet wet and see how it runs out on the long haul road. We already knew the Sportster was just fine, cuz I had given it the Torture Test on the Canada trip. And we also had one other little Virgin Cherry to pop,… Freddie's!

Cuz he hadn't been out on a camping bike trip yet, either. So this was new to both Freddie and the Super Glide. We packed the road gear on the Harleys and took off. It was an uneventful trip just stopping for gas and eats along the way, until we got down close to Galveston. And then, us two Texas kids who had been born and raised there all our lives, ran into something,…literally,…that we had never seen before.

The speed limit back then was 55, so we were probably doin' 55 or maybe 60. And up ahead across the entire road we saw this black mist,…kinda like an undulating black fog, slowly moving along the road, changing shapes as it drifted. What the hell was it? Was it some diesel smoke from some 18 wheeler up ahead or maybe some smoke from a farm tractor that was off the side of the road?

Nope. It was bugs! Millions and millions of bugs. We rode right through them and got slimed like you wouldn't believe, bwahaha! I mean, if two firemen had been standing on each side of the road when we rode by and they aimed their hoses at us and sprayed us with snot, that is what it was like,…gross!

We had them slimey gooey yellow green bug guts all over us and both Harleys. We had to pull off the road it was soooo fuckin' bad, hahaha. Those fuckin' bugs went all inside our helmets,…helmet law back then,…and they went up our noses and in our eyes and were crawlin' around inside our ears. We had to yank off our helmets and try to clean the green slime goop off as best we could,…which wasn't very good. Now I don't know which is worse. To get hit with mushy gooey bug guts all over you, or to hit one of them June bugs with the hard shell so fast that when it hits you in the forehead, it feels like you got shot in the head.

The next mom & pop gas station we stopped at, the bikes still had the bug guts all over 'em. And when we asked the older guy about them bugs, he just laughed at us, like we were 'Yankees from up Dallas Way', hahaha. He sez, "Don't you boys know what them bugs are? Them's Love Bugs." I asked him "Whaddaya mean Love Bugs? What's that?" He sez "That's what you just hit. Them bugs like to fuck in mid air, see? And when they are fuckin' in mid air, nuthin' stops 'em. So they fly around hooked up in all them groups, two by two until somebody like you hits and kills 'em." Hmm. Oh joy. So now we have been educated about Love Bugs, the hard way and I still remember hittin' them squishy things 48 years later. Anyhow, the rest of the trip was really fun with nice weather and we rode mostly around the Galveston area by the palm trees and down the Gulf a bit.

We stayed our 2 nights out for the 3 day weekend we made, then hauled ass back to Dallas the last day to get back to our jobs. So that weekend gave the 74 Super Glide and Freddie a good old fashioned cherry bustin' 600 to 700 mile ride and nothin' broke on Freddie or the Super Glide,…just yet,…but it did still have the wobbly pulsating rear disc brake which was very annoying.

THE EARLY YEARS

FALL OF 1973 TO JULY 11, 1974

Part 1:

After the Calgary Alberta Road Trip was over, I settled down to work helping build the 7/10ths of one-mile-long banana shaped Braniff Terminal at the DFW Airport. It was a crazy overtime job, which meant kinda big paychecks for me, an 18 year old kid just entering Carpenter Apprentice School. I was making a whoppin' $4.01 an hour, hahaha. But that sure beat the $1.65 an hour I'd been gettin' flippin' burgers at Jack in the Box, and it beat the hell outta washing dishes and pumping gas for a $1.00 an hour.

But all was not rosy on the home front. My good ol' dad was still ticked off that I went against his orders and got the Sportster. After all, he had told me 'no kid of mine is gonna live in my house and ride a motorcycle.' Gulp. But instead of givin' me the boot to the curb, he charged me rent to live there in my room,…25 bucks a week.

Now I mighta just been 18 years old, but I could still kinda do math, and that 25 bucks a week to me added up to 100 bucks a month to live at home. Wow. Kinda harsh, eh? However, looking back I'm glad he did that, cuz it gave me the guts to hurry up and go out on my own. In a few months with the nice overtime paychecks from the airport job, I wound up getting my own 2 bedroom house with a 1 car garage out back for $12,500 and the payments were $104 a month, just 4 bucks more than I had been paying to live at home.

And years later I found out that the folks' mortgage on the house they built back in 1949 was 66 bucks a month, so he was charging me almost double what his house payment was. Try that with your kid today and they'll bust you for child abuse, hah. Meanwhile, I had also gotten my first car off a used car lot in Arlington, a Red 1968 Mustang for 1,800 bucks and was making payments on it and it could haul my tools in its trunk,…yay.

So going into the winter of 1973 I had the Red 67 Sportster, the Red 68 Mustang and my own house. When I got the Mustang, it was totally stock, so as quick as I could I added the High Jacker Air Shocks, Cragar mags with raised white letter tires and a new dual exhaust.

In the spring of 1974, I turned 19 and realized my 6-foot 3 frame was kinda too big for the Sportster, so I started making plans and saving money for a new Super Glide. I had a high school buddy named Freddie who wanted the Red Sportster and I told him the instant I could save 1500 bucks, he could have it for 1500 bucks and that would cash me out for the new Super Glide. So we made the deal and it happened in the end of May, I sold Freddie the 67 Sportster for the 1500 bucks, and I had another 1500 bucks ready to go down to the Harley dealer and get my new Super Glide.

Only one problem,…the factory was on their AMF Strike and there wasn't one single Super Glide at any of the four Dallas-Fort Worth dealers,…yikes! So now I got the cash but got no bike.

Bummer. I had to pay 100 bucks down at Conley's and Harry Hines Harley dealers in Dallas to get on their waiting lists, then another 100 bucks at Ivey's HD in Grand Prairie, then another 100 bucks down at Chandler's HD in Fort Worth. Day after day ticked by with no word on any new bikes coming in. I wasn't even being picky, I didn't care if I got an FX or an FXE, didn't even care what color it was, but I was hoping for either black or purple.

Then one Saturday night in June, I had been over in Arlington shootin' pool. On the way back home I drove by Ivey's Harley dealership to see if any new bikes had come in yet. Nope.

BUT WAIT! What's that over there? My beer infused eyeballs finally focused in on something new-ish sittin' there on the showroom floor underneath the lights.

And that somethin' new was a Black 1972 Super Glide! Now I never cared much for the 1971 Boat Tail Super Glide versions, but the 72 was a different critter altogether. And this one I was now lookin' at was even better than the stock version. This 72 Super Glide still had its Fat Bob tanks, plus it had Red Pinstriping…plus…it already had a +6 inch over stock glide front end on it. And 1972 was the year before them fuckin' disc brakes came out, so that means it had the old style Sportster drum brake on it. I was shocked! There sat my dream bike, all ready for me to ride off on. I could already envision myself going down the road on it. It also had a price tag hangin' off its handlebars and that price tag read $2500. So it was gonna be 500 or 600 less than the new bikes which weren't to be had anyhow,…yippee! And I even had the pile of cash sittin' at home to get it. What more could I ask for?

Well, there was one problem. This was late on Saturday night and they were closed until Monday morning and I had to go to work Monday morning so I made the fateful decision to get it Monday evening after work. What could possibly go wrong with that,…right?

I drove back down to the dealer Sunday afternoon while they were still closed and I stared at it some more through the window,… lickin' my chops just like a hungry wolf salivatin' over a nice tender little sheepie. I talked to Freddie that night and asked him if he could gimme a ride over to get my new 72 Super Glide, he said sure. Since it was not a brand new bike, they didn't hafta do all that dealer prep crap to it, I should be able to pay 'em the loot in cash, sign the papers, and start the sucker up and ride away, right? Sounds simple enough.

Went to work Monday and all I could think about was that beautiful 1972 Black Super Glide waitin' for me at Ivey's. Got off work and Freddie came by on the (now his) Red 67 Sportster. That meant I was gonna hafta ride bitch all the way over to the dealer, kinda embarrassing, but I'm going after that new bike and Freddie and me can ride together when I get it and head back home with it. That will be my first ride on the 72, ridin' along with Freddie and lookin' at the ol' 67 Sportster going up and down the road. Seemed cool enough to me, so ridin' bitch wasn't all that bad,…or was it?

If you've ever ridden on the back section of an old timey Sportster Cobra Seat, you know they ain't got much paddin', or much support, or much room, or not much of anything else, hahaha. They just look cool, that's all. It was like sittin' on a little postage stamp back there. I had put the little 10 inch sissy bar on it the year before when the 67 was mine, and that was all that I had to lean back on and hold on to. Plus, Freddie was about 6 foot tall and I was 3 inches taller than him, and the back fender sits up higher than the front part of the seat. So Freddie probably looked normal sittin' on there and then there I am on the back, ridin' up high on the rear fender like Herman Munster.

And with both of our weight on the Sportster, that means we had loaded the suspension to its stretching point, so it was a kinda rough ride without much spring and shock action. But that's still OK, cuz I'm sittin' back there ridin' bitch, bitin' the bullet, cuz at the end of this miserable ride I know I'm gettin' that Black 72 Shovelhead. And then we came up to a bunch of potholes at an intersection and the light turned yellow cuz it was goin' red.

Now if I had been ridin' in the front seat, I'da twisted that Sportster's throttle and made it through the light just in the nick of time. But I ain't the one controlling the throttle. Nope. So what does Freddie do? He slams on the brakes without me being ready, and we hit them potholes with the Sportster's bottomed out suspension, and that means I slid forward real fast and bruised both my plums up against his back and I let out a painful howl and Freddie started laughing, hahahaha. Umm,...dude,...it ain't funny. Or,...is it? I guess it was kinda funny as long as you weren't me, or my crunched gonads, hahaha. So now that I can hit the high notes like a Eunuch Choir, the light turned green and we rode the rest of the way to Ivey's with no further bad incidents. The next bad incident didn't happen until we got there.

So Freddie pulled us into Ivey's parking lot and I jumped off,...gingerly with still bruised plums,...and I swung open that front door and waltzed in to claim my new prize. Only problem? It wasn't there. I figgered they musta took it in the back to do an oil change or check the battery, shit like that. Then I called out to Harvey Ivey over at his parts counter, "Hey Harvey, where's that Black Super Glide you had sittin' in here over the weekend?" Harvey sez,... "Sold it."

WHAT?! Yep, he had sold it before I got there and the bike of my dreams is now gone,...forever. The word "disappointed" doesn't come even halfway close to the gnawin' empty pain in my gut that I was feeling right then. All my weekend's worth of dreams now shattered. So Freddie and me went back out to the 67 Sportster so's I could have my humiliatin' bitch ride back home. Sigh.

Then a coupla days later after I got off work, I was headed out to gobble some food in the Red 68 Mustang cuz that's all the wheels I had, and I drove up to the end of my street and then I turned left to go downtown,...when,... THERE IT IS! There's the Black 1972 Super Glide with the Red Pinstripes and the 6 inch over front end with the old Sportster drum brake on it, right at the end of my very own street, parked in front of a neighbor's house, HOLY SHIT! I pulled the Mustang over, hopped out and went up and knocked on the front door. This guy my size opens the door and I asked him if that was his bike and he said yep, he just got it. Turns out this guy was named Ray and he was 20 years old and had a brand new beautiful wife named Debra, and we hit it off just fine. Of course, it was easy for Ray to hit it off cuz he was happy and ridin' the koolest Super Glide in town while I ain't got no motorsickle,...sniff, sniff.

And I must put in this part of the story. Ray was orange. Yep, he was orange, and he smelled good enough to lick and bite. Why? Cuz he worked for Frito/Lay's in Dallas and Ray was the guy who ran the machine that put the orange barbeque flavored stuff on the Lay's barbeque potato chips, hahaha. What a cool job, eh? All ya needed was Barbequed Ray and a 6 pack and there ya go, snack time.

Ray and Debra were kind enough to search and search through their old photos and they found this really good one, both of 'em on "my" ol' 1972 Super Glide, toolin' on up the highway. Ray told me I took this picture of them on our road trip to Galveston then gave it to them. So I ain't seen this photo since 1974-ish. And meanwhile, it's gettin' to the end of June and I'm still waitin' on a Super Glide to come in,...somewhere.

Then on Wednesday afternoon July 10, 1974… I got 'The Phone Call' from Ivey's HD in Grand Prairie to come down and get my new Super Glide if I still wanted it. Harvey Ivey told me I was not the next guy up on his list. Then he told me that he had been trying to contact the guy in front of me, but could not get a-hold of him. So Harvey said if I got down there with the cash, the bike was mine. I drove the Mustang down there as fast as I could without getting a ticket, hah. And when I walked into the shop, we went to the back room and there it was, a brand new Black FXE, still sitting in the

2X4 crate, right next to an Electra Glide still in its crate. I wish I'da had a camera then to take its picture, but I didn't own one yet.

But,...there was a problem. Look at that Electra Glide,...it's fucked up. It has half a black fat bob tank and the other half has the purple color I also liked. There was a note taped to the gas tank. It read "I get paid $8.20 an hour to fuck up motorcycles. How much do you get paid to find out what I did?"

So now Harvey had to have Tiny and his other mechanic go through the two new bikes and see what was up. Mine turned out to be OK, (they claimed) but the Electra Glide had a 9/16ths wrench inside the primary cover. Think what that woulda done if they'da fired it up? Anyhow, on Thursday July 11, 1974, I became the original owner of the 1974 Shovelhead I still ride today. Here's a photo from back then I took with my folks' camera. Freddie's back there on the 67 Sportster, looking like he's bored ready to go ridin' while I'm taking this picture.

1974 Super Glide Woes

Part 2:

After getting the Super Glide from the dealer, I thought I now had a brand-new trouble-free bike to do road trips on. Man, was I wrong. From the first day, every time I hit the back brake, which was a fairly new disc brake idea back then, the back wheel and brake pedal pulsated. Like it grabbed and let go, grabbed and let go, really fast, and it would actually make my foot feel like it was going up and down on the brake pedal. I talked to the dealer about it. He said "Just give it some time and a few miles and let it break in." OK.

Next thing? When I pushed the starter button, it would make a grinding clicking sizzling noise and a cloud of gray smoke would come up from down there, somewhere.

So then I'd try to kick the fucker. And when I'd kick the kicker down, it would fire up,…maybe,…and then when I took my foot off the kicker, it would come back up into position and then just keep unwinding, cuz inside the kicker cover on the kicker gear, that little pawl would bust off, so there was nothing to stop the kicker arm from unwinding, see? So the kicker arm would be hanging down, not in an upright position. And I already had lots of experience kicking over the 67 Sportster, so it wasn't like I was new at this kicking shit.

Meanwhile,…the rear brake kept pulsating.

Then the 3 circuit breakers under the headlight nacelle would go out, right in the middle of traffic sometimes on the way to apprentice school, and the bike would die right where ever we happened to be. Then I'd bang my fist on top of the headlight to jar the breakers and then they'd fire back up,…most of the time.

There were also 3 circuit breakers under the seat and they would also go out and kill the bike, so I'd hafta coast and pull over, get off, raise the seat up, then wiggle those 3 breakers and kick it to see if it would start again. Most of the time it would.

Meanwhile,…the rear brake kept pulsating.

Then there was that little chrome box up in front of the motor, they called it the "Rectifier/Regulator Module" and I had 3 of those damn things burn up in the first 6 months I owned the bike. Those little suckers were 84 bucks a pop. My fuckin' house payment was 104, so that 84 bucks was outrageous in my view.

Oh,…and guess how long of a warranty they gave me for the new $3,000 bike? 3 months, that's it. Yes, three months not a typo. One day after I had the bike for maybe 6 months and the rear brake was still pulsating, I went in to the dealer REALLY pissed off cuz the caliper on the rear brake had kinda let loose, and it fell down onto the top of the rotor and got hot from all the spinning friction and then the fucker got sooo hot it locked up the rear wheel on me in freeway traffic, skidded me over to the shoulder and then I dropped the bike in the weeds. All because of that fuckin' disc brake on back. I had to wait until the fucker cooled down so I could fire it back up and ride home really slow, trying not to heat the fucker up again. Brand-new trouble-free bike, eh?

So now my 19-year-old ass is livid, yelling at the guys in Ivey's. There just happened to be an audience for this tirade, a guy in a suit and tie standing at the parts counter watching me come unhinged. It was my lucky day. He told the guys to pull off the back rotor and see if it was flat or not. They did what he told them, and then came back out and said "That rotor is warped, you need a new one." I yelled out "OH REALLY? You mean just like I've been saying from the first fucking day I got this piece of shit? You guys probably knew it all along, you were just waiting for my warranty to expire so you could charge me for it, right?"

Then the suit & tie guy at the parts counter told them to give me a new brake system, rotor, caliper, pads, the whole enchilada, cuz that guy just happened to be a factory rep and it was my lucky day he was there. And that's why we called these earlier 1970s AMF

Shovelheads "A Mother Fucker" cuz that is exactly what they were, hahaha. And when I'd ride it over to the folks' house and then get ready to leave, my dad would be standing there while I was kicking and he'd say "Don't start. Don't start. Don't start." Then he'd laugh at me, hahaha. And the electric start never worked.

Part 3: 1974 AMF,... Gettin' the Bugs Out?

After having to fuck with and fuck with and fuck with this bike soooo much, I was starting to get really pissed off at it. Can ya believe that? At first I was telling myself, 'hey, it ain't the bike's fault, it is just a piece of machinery that needs some TLC and was built by some pissed off people that didn't care what they did.'

Yep,...that's what I told myself,...at first. But then I came to realize the truth. This 1974 AMF Super Glide FXE was in fact a demon possessed piece of shit. It fuckin' hated my guts, hahaha. But I was determined to make the piece of shit work. After all, I got rid of the nice 67 Sportster for a more comfortable road bike, right? One that would fit my frame and not have me all cramped up on the pegs.

But now I had a piece of AMF shit that I was afraid to ride anywhere. I knew it was gonna die on me, somewhere, somehow. And I had my dad laughing at me for getting it in the first place, and then I had some guys at Brown's and Shelby's shop telling me shit like 'I told you that you shoulda gotten a Panhead chopper for the same price but you wouldn't listen to me." Oh, just great, eh?

Anyhow, as the months went by and it got to be spring of 1975, I kinda had the bugs sorted out,...maybe. And it was at this time that I said 'fuck it' to having any dealer ever touch my bike again, cuz they scratched up the paint on the back end of the swing arm when they did the rear brake fix, and then the guy lied about it to the owner and the owner took his mechanic's word over mine. So fuck 'em. And no dealer ever did anything for me since that day, except for when Joe Cox did my motor a few years later in the winter of 1979. But I was using Joe to do the build cuz he was Joe Cox, one of the best motor builders in Dallas-Fort Worth. I used Joe in spite of him being there at the HD dealer, not because he was there.

Now it was getting to be spring time of 1975 and that meant my 18 year old Baby Brudder was getting ready to grad-u-ma-gate from high school. And you might not ever guess what my dad got him for his graduation present. I got a Number 4 Stanley Plane when I got outta high school. What do ya'll think my little brudder got? (Hint: It has 2 wheels)

Here is the 74 AMF Piece of Shit and 20-year-old me in early spring, 1975.

The 1975 Road Trip

Part 1: "Here's the Riders"

In 1975 my little brudder was 18 and just gettin' outta high school and he wound up gettin' a nice used 1971 Shovelhead that he got from a guy that took off the dresser front end and stuck this one on. I called him my "little" brudder but at 6 foot 4 he was bigger than my 6 foot 3, hahaha. And you don't ever wanna get in his way when he's eatin', cuz it's all forks and knives and elbows goin' everywhere. Believe you me, how do ya think he got bigger'n me?

Now our 'Plan for Fun' we had been plannin' to do was a cross country multi state motorsickle trip together ridin' through mountains and stuff. Our 19 year old Cuzzin Johnny was gonna join in on the action, too. My high school buddy Freddie that bought the old 67 Sportster from me had to work his fairly new job, so he couldn't go, and our other Cuzzin Paul who went on the Dallas to Calgary 1973 Road Trip had gotten outta college and started a new job so he couldn't go, either. So my Brudder Charles and me were packing up to go.

Our Double Cuzzin Johnny was riding in to Dallas from Ardmore Oklahoma to start out with us, too. What is a Double Cuzzin? Well now, it might sound a bit incestuous, but it ain't. No really, it ain't, hahaha. Our dad and Johnny's dad were brothers, see? And our mom and Johnny's mom were sisters, see? So two brothers married two sisters, and our folks had 3 boys and they had 3 boys so it was kinda like there were 6 of us, all kinda close to the same age.

Anyhow this is #60, my Brudder Charles with his 1971 Shovel and we are gettin' ready to roll out in just a few more minutes.

THE EARLY YEARS

The 1975 Road Trip

Part 2: "Here's the Riders"

After my 18 year old Baby Brudder, next up on the group of riders was our 19 year old Cuzzin Johnny, who lived in Oklahoma. He got his Norton at Storm's Cycles on the west end of Dallas by the old Highway 80. Storm's sold Nortons and Moto Guzzis. For some reason unknown to me, the shop that sold Triumphs and BSAs was on up the hill closer to downtown Dallas.

Anyhow, this Norton here was a special bike. Storm's built it themselves. The motor is the last year of the 750s, so that must be a 1972? And the frame was the first year of the 850 frames, so I'm guessing it's a 1973 frame? Johnny got it from Storm's in 1974.

So for this June 1975 Road Trip, Cuzzin Johnny rode it down from Oklahoma and our dad made a bracket to go on the Norton's sissy bar to strap a back pack to. Johnny ain't in this photo but he is in the one when we ride back to the Oklahoma border to get his gear. Johnny is a big ol' boy, too. Probably 6 foot solid and maybe 215 pounds. Johnny is the kinda kid that if you wanted somebody to pick up your refrigerator and throw it across your front yard, he could probably do it for you. I used to think Charles and Johnny shoulda been pro rasslers and I coulda been their sneaky manager, hittin' the other guys with chairs when Charles and Johnny bounced them outta the ring.

On this trip when we walked into cafes, gas stations, diners or whatever, some of the folks' heads would jerk around kinda quick like 3 Bigfoots just walked in. One guy at a gas station in Colorado thought we were from the Dallas Cowboys, hahaha.

THE EARLY YEARS

The 1975 Road Trip

Part 3: "Here's the Riders"

And last and smallest, we've got 20 year old me and the ol' 74 AMF Shovelhead and some of you may recognize it's got some custom paint at this stage. Why is that? Cuz in early 1975 I was doing woodwork at Six Flags Over Texas, over in Arlington. I'd do repair work on the wooden roller coaster arms, hang doors and do hardware, built a big 22 foot diameter water wheel for the place with the big stage called The Music Mill where acts like Kris Kristofferson and Chuck Berry played. A stream of water in the wooden flume turned the big water wheel and it looked like the mill was working while the musicians played inside it, pretty cool, actually. And I'd make the big sandwich sign boards that the sign painters would paint. So here comes the tank work. Will Patterson was the premier sign painter at Six Flags and he is the guy that painted the murals on the 74's gas tank. Up on top it has a lace job with Champagne Bubbles and crazy multi colored air brush work, like an acid trip. On the sides it has desert scenes.

Anyhow, when school let out, that meant Brudder Charles was outta school now, and Six Flags opened up to the public, and that meant I got laid off, so it was Road Trip Time, bwahahaha. Here is the 74 Super Glide all packed up for the road. Now we're off to Oklahoma to get Cuzzin Johnny's road gear.

THE EARLY YEARS

The 1975 Road Trip

Part 4: "Ridin' to Ardmore"

So, the three cuzzins started up their motorsickles in Dallas and took out headed for Oklahoma, Cuzzin Johnny's homeland. We rode up I-35 through Denton and Gainesville. On the way to Oklahoma, we rode over the Red River, which is the border between Oklahoma and Texas. If some of you ain't never seen the Red River,… well lemme tell ya,…it's red. Really red. It has red banks, red sand down on the bottom and all the water runnin' through it is red. So that name fits pretty good, eh? And when we were kids, we heard some rumors that Red River had some of that quicksand stuff in it, so I never ventured down there to find out for myself if it really did or not. I remember watching Tarzan movies and knew what quicksand can do, hahaha.

After we crossed Red River we rode through Marietta which is in Love County. As a side note, Charles' and my folks got married there on Valentine's Day in Love County, how romantic, eh? Marietta also had the Little Brownie Cookie Shop where our folks used to pull the old 1950 Mercury into the parking lot so's we could get fresh baked cookies to take to our grandfolks' house and share with the cuzzins, and we also got to help ourselves to the Free Samples in the big cookie jar at the front counter. Imagine that action today? Of course not, hahaha. That's why it was sooo much fun being kids back then in the 1960s. And this is the Oklahoma border sign and our next stop up will be Cuzzin Johnny's house on up the road a piece.

THE EARLY YEARS

The 1975 Road Trip

Part 5: "Gettin' to Ardmore"

We left off last time where I was taking the picture of Brudder Charles and Cuzzin Johnny at the Oklahoma Border Sign after we just rode over the Red River Bridge, which is the state line. Marietta is the first town of any size that you run into, and from there Ardmore is about 20 more miles up the road.

We made it to Cuzzin Johnny's house just fine, so far no breakdowns in our first 2 hours on the road trip, hahaha. So that's good. While Johnny was inside packing up his tent, sleeping bag and other road gear to strap on his Snortin' Norton, his gal friend Janie showed up with a bag of fresh cookies she had made.

Now this might sound kinda terrible, but it's what happened and I never stray from what actually happened. I am sorta speculatin' now that Janie made those cookies for Her Beloved, and she mighta had visions of him out underneath the stars at night with the campfire gently going, occasional pops and snaps from the wood in the fire, reflecting off the chrome from his Norton in the camp fire light. Maybe she thought as Cuzzin Johnny took a bite from each delicious handmade cookie, he'd remember how she made those with her own lovin' hands just for him. That could very well be close to the romantic little plan she had.

But what actually happened is Charles and me saw 'em too, and that entire bag of cookies was gone before we left the driveway. Burp. Ain't that terrible? I took this picture of Johnny and Janie standing by his Snortin' Norton's sissy bar, and maybe Janie ain't really happy with me at this point? We are gettin' ready to roll out now.

THE EARLY YEARS

The 1975 Road Trip

Part 6: "Off to Turner Falls"

Cuzzin Johnny's Norton and Brudder Charles' 71 Shovelhead and my 74 Shovelhead all pulled outta Johnny's folks' driveway and we headed on through the city streets until we got to the main road and took off for the Arbuckle Mountains to see the nice waterfalls called Turner Falls, our next stop. It was only about a half hour away. Turner Falls is a purdy big waterfalls on Honey Creek in the Arbuckles. It's about 77 feet high and considered to be one of the highest waterfalls in Oklahoma.

And we made it there, On the left we have #60 Charles and on the right is #73 Johnny. That's a lotta beef on the hoof right there, lemme tell ya.

The 1975 Road Trip

Part 7: "First Night Camping"

We started up the three motorsickles and took off from Turner Falls in the Arbuckle Mountains. From Turner Falls we kept going up I-35 to Oklahoma City. There used to be a long left hand sweeper onto I-40 just south of downtown OKC. Suddenly my bike was dead. Charles and Johnny said they rode on a mile or so before they noticed, NO DAVID!!

They said they backtracked and found me on the shoulder in the middle of the turn fiddling with a dead 1974 AMF Harley. The three circuit breakers under the seat had pulled their little cute trick again, hahaha, so I wiggled them until they worked and we were back on our way pretty quickly.

I-40 splits Oklahoma in half north and south. We camped at Red Rock Canyon State Park near Hinton where, of course, it rained. We didn't care though, we were on an adventure. And it had already gotten dark by the time we pulled into the campground and got our tent spots. Now since Charles was only 18 and Johnny was 19, and since 20 year old me was The Elder of our group and since I had already been on a long cross country trip from Dallas to Calgary, I took it upon myself 'to learn these young whippersnappers' how to set up a tent really quick. Like, "Ya'll just watch me and I'll show ya how it's done fast."

I laid my orange pup tent down on the ground and spread out all 4 corners nice and flat. Then I took the 4 stakes and staked out the corners really quick-like, see? (I'm giving 'em an un- asked for demonstration.) Then I took the tent pole and put it together, looped it through the loop on the front of the tent, stood it up, then looped the line over the tent pole, walked backward with it nice and tight and staked it into the ground, so now the front of the tent is standing. See how simple it is, hahaha? And then?

And then I put the other tent pole together, walked to the back of my tent, looped the tent pole through the loop in the top of the tent, and then I started walking backwards with it to tighten it up good,…when,… WHOA! WHOOPS! KER-SPLASH! Right down the bank and into the creek I went, getting drenched, bwahahaha! We had no idea there was a creek there, cuz it was dark. Even my boots got soaked. So there I am, climbing up the muddy bank, all embarrassed to shit, soaked good and muddy, with Charles and Johnny laughing their asses off at me, hahaha! What a great start to the road trip, eh? All my shit's wet the first night out, hahaha.

So what did I do next? Well, I pulled out the little 15 dollar cheapie Kodak Instamatic camera and took this here crummy photo. It's blurry and dark and out of focus and it captures that hilarious motorsickle camping moment in 1975 just perfect if ya ask me. And when I took this picture, Johnny asks "Why are you taking all these pictures?" And I sez, "So when we are old and gray, we can look back at these pictures and remember the fun motorsickle trip we took when we were kids."

The 1975 Road Trip

Part 8: "Back Across Texas"

We broke camp the next morning, packed up the three motor-sickles, stopped to get gas and eat breakfast and took off west again,…and my boots were still wet from falling in the water, hahaha. We were now headed back across the top of Texas to get over to New Mexico. Here's the picture Cuzzin Johnny took of Charles and me at the Texas Border with Charles' 1971 Shovelhead.

The 1975 Road Trip

Part 9: "Route 66"

Once we rode back into the Texas Panhandle from Oklahoma, we caught the Mother Road, Route 66 and headed on into Alanreed, which is about 40 miles or so into Texas on Route 66.

Now what's in Alanreed you might ask? Oh,…lot's of cool stuff, for what some folks might consider to be a Ghost Town. It's the old territory for the Comanche and Kiowa tribes. It's got the oldest church and cemetery along Route 66. And the old antique sign going into town read:

Alanreed City Limits Population: 52 People
104 Dogs
88 Cats
2 Skunks
And a Few Snakes

Snakes? Now who doesn't love those cute little poisonous killer rattlesnakes and lizards, right? So we just had to pull the three motor-sickles in to take a look at the Regal Reptile Ranch. We had to. And you woulda done it too, right? Of course, cuz this is Americana at its best.

THE EARLY YEARS

The 1975 Road Trip

Part 10: "Texas Panhandle"

After we left the Regal Reptile Ranch, we kept ridin' on the old Route 66 as we headed toward Amarillo out in the Texas Panhandle where that big ranch is with all those Cadillacs buried on their front ends. They call it the Cadillac Ranch, and it's a public art sculpture outside Amarillo that was done in 1974 by Chip Lord, Doug Michels, and Hudson Marquez who were members of an art group called Ant Farm. And this trip was in 1975 so the Cadillac Ranch was still kinda new at the time. Today, nearly 50 years later, all the Caddys have been vandalized and graffitied to death. Oh well. That's some hard-core art for ya, hah.

Since we were just ridin' along out there sorta in the middle of nowhere, Brudder Charles wanted to take some kinda action shot. So he pulled over to the side of the road and told me to ride back up the highway and then back to him and do something, so I did. He took this one of me coming up the highway. And if ya look close, I think that is an old Stuckey's yellow billboard out there in the background. Remember when you are riding to always be safe and keep both hands on the handlebars at all times, OK?

THE EARLY YEARS

The 1975 Road Trip

Part 11: "Ridin' Into New Mexico"

From the Amarillo Texas Panhandle area out on Route 66 you got about 2 hours or so to ride to Tucumcari New Mexico, and Tucumcari is the largest city you run into on Route 66 going from Amarillo to Albuquerque. They say Tucumcari has the largest number of original old Route 66 vintage feelings and buildings on the ride. Tucumcari still had their wonderful old vintage gas stations, diners, motels, lounges, and cafes with the original vintage neon signs. If you can name it, they got it Old Skool Route 66 Style.

Ridin' the Norton and two Shovelheads through downtown Tucumcari was like being transported back in time to the 1950s and '60s. But before we got to Tucumcari, we stopped at the border and clumb up on this New Mexico border sign for a Photo Op, just so's you could see it right now. We got #60 Cuzzin Johnny up on the right side and that's yours truly up on the left and Brudder Charles snapped the picture. And no, I ain't a-gonna try to climb up it these days unless you gimme a ladder.

Now,…here's a very strange trivia for those of you who have been following this road trip drivel oh-so-closely. When we left Oklahoma, Johnny was #73 and Charles was #60,…so what happened? I dunno, you tell me, hahaha.

THE EARLY YEARS

THE 1975 ROAD TRIP

Part 12: "Ridin' Into Tucumcari"

So after climbin' up on the border sign and gettin' our picture made without even bustin' the sign down, we rode on into Tucumcari, New Mexico.

Now, please excuse me for this picture part, cuz I have used this Tucumcari gas station photo before, cuz unfortunately it is the only Tucumcari photo I have. Randal and me stopped in at this very same gas station on our road trip, but we hit it coming the other way, ridin' from the west to east, going from Albuquerque to Amarillo.

THE EARLY YEARS

This time Charles and Johnny and me hit this same gas station coming into Tucumcari from the east, headed on our way up north to Colorado to ride up Pikes Peak. After we took this gas stop picture, we went into one of the old downtown turquoise shops and got us some turquoise rings, think 1975 David Alan Coe. And yes, I still have my ring today and I believe Brudder Charles has his, too. And over on another street corner, there was a plywood enclosure that was fulla rattlesnakes and they had a sign there sayin' it was good luck if you could drop a coin on a rattlesnake's head, hahaha.

THE 1975 ROAD TRIP

Part 13: "Got to Tucumcari"

After putting in a full day's ride in crazy cross winds, and after getting rained on the night before when we were camping in Oklahoma, we three motorsickle jockeys got a nice motel room at the Palomino Motel in Tucumcari.

And get this, it was only 15 bucks for the night, that's right, 5 measly bucks each, hahaha. AND,…they had a swimming pool, which felt good cuz the desert area had been kinda warmish that day. We ate at a little cowboy lookin' joint across the street that night. This is our little rag tag group in the motel parking lot.

The 1975 Road Trip

Part 14: "Ridin' Across New Mexico"

From Tucumcari we rode on some little highways (maybe Highway 54 to 39 up to I-25?) headed north to Raton, New Mexico and then Trinidad, Colorado. I remember it being really windy, so windy in fact that we were leaning to our left into the monster wind outta the west for a looooong time. The next gas stop we joked about how the left side of our tires would be worn out before the right side was.

This is a shot of our three motorsickles out there in the desert area. Road looks kinda lonely, don't it? But it's still purdy and it looks like it was a nice clear day with just a few fluffy clouds up there,… which sure beats the rain.

The 1975 Road Trip

Part 15: "Headed to Colorado"

Here are three shots out kinda in the desert area of northern New Mexico. We got Brudder Charles on his 71 Shovel on the side of the road, our bikes parked on the side of the road while we stretched our legs and some desolate looking turf in the other one.

The 1975 Road Trip

Part 16: "Colorado"

Yay! We made it to the Colorado Border. Charles took this picture of Johnny and me at the border sign and you can see that 55 Speed Limit sign in the background. Charles told us he had a rather narrow escape on the road going maybe a little bit too fast into a corner with the cross-wind gusts getting to him. He said he thought he nearly lost it, but made it OK. Now on to Pikes Peak.

What number jersey has Cuzzin Johnny got on this time?

The 1975 Road Trip

Part 17: "Ridin' to Pikes Peak"

When we got into Colorado, I remember us three motorsickle jockeys pulling in to a gas station that had a diner next door. We gassed up the bikes and went in the diner to eat. We squeezed into a booth and the waitress came to take our orders.

Johnny and Charles ordered their food, then I ordered my burger and I asked the waitress if they could 'cut the onions.' A few minutes later she brought our food out and when she set my burger down in front of me, she also set down a plate fulla chopped up little onion pieces, I said "What is that?" She sez "You told me to cut the onions, so we did."

Hmm,...whaddaya know about that shit, eh? So I told her "No, I didn't want any onions at all on it. So how do you order a burger here without onions?" She looks at me like she was ready to say 'kiss my grits' like Flo in Mel's Diner and then she rolls her eyes and sez "We say I'd like a hamburger without onions." BWAHAHAHA!

Well that was a good 'un on me, eh? Ya see, when I was 16 years old I flipped burgers at Jack in the Box, and whenever anybody wanted a burger without onions, they'd yell back to me on the grill, "and cut the onions" so that stuck with me all that time. Anyway, here's a picture of the Colorado territory as we're sneakin' up on Pikes Peak.

By 1975 our Cuzzin Peggy had moved from Colorado Springs to California, so we didn't get to stop in and see her on this trip.

THE EARLY YEARS

THE 1975 ROAD TRIP

Part 18: "Ridin' up The Big Bump"

While it was maybe 80 degrees or so down on the bottom land at the start, the higher we rode up Pikes Peak, the colder it got. And back in 1975, the road was not paved like it was later. We were on a dirt road. And to think how Al Unser and them guys used to race up this hill? Holy shit, hahaha. One look over the side can take your breath away. In some spots, it's a looooong ways down to the bottom. This is the type of terrain we were in. And all three motorsickles were runnin' just fine all the way to the top, even when it got colder.

The 1975 Road Trip

Part 19: "Pikes Peak Summit"

The Norton Commando and the two Harley Shovelheads kept pluggin' along right on up the big mountain and next thing we knew,…we were freezin' our asses off with snow all around us, hahaha. Oh. And we eventually made it to the top.

While Charles and Johnny were kinda thinkin' ahead and had on their nice warm coats with the fleece linings in 'em, I was wearing my buckskin fringe Billy jacket and freezin' half to death, hah. But hey, at least I had the fringes blowin' in the wind, right? So I had that goin' for me, which was nice. So here we are, the three double cuzzins at 14,110 feet high.

The 1975 Road Trip

Part 20: "Pikes Peak Summer Snow"

We were three southern boys from Texas and Oklahoma who had been raised in areas without much snow, so when we got up on top of Pikes Peak we played around in it for a little while. After all, we spent maybe 3 hours or so riding up to the top on the gravel road, then ya gotta spend another 3 hours or so riding back down. It eats up most of the day doing Pikes Peak rides, so we gotta spend more than 15 or 20 minutes on top, even if it was cold,…right?

Here's three photos of us cuzzins up on the summit, Brudder Charles standin' in the snow looking way back down from where we had ridden up, Cuzzin Johnny buried knee deep in the white stuff, and me a-layin' in the cold stuff.

THE EARLY YEARS

The 1975 Road Trip

Part 21: "Top of Pikes Peak"

Before us three Norton Commando and Harley Shovelhead cuzzins climbed on the motorsickles and headed back down the gravel road to the base of Pikes Peak, I rode mine over to the edge maybe kinda where ya ain't supposed to go and took this last photo of it up on top of Pikes Peak. Now at this stage, after all the bullshit this Summer of 1974 Strike Built AMF Shovelhead had put me through in the past year, I coulda given it just one big righteous kick or push and sent it crashing over the edge to the jagged rocks down below.

And just think how many millions of dollars that woulda saved me from doing all those 7 bare frame up chopper builds on it over the next 47 years, hahaha. But nooooo, I had to keep it instead. "Til Death Do Us Part."

THE 1975 ROAD TRIP

Part 22: "Manitou Springs, Colorado"

After we rode the Norton and two Shovelheads down from the 14,110 foot Pikes Peak Summit, we were good and hon-gry and we stopped in at Manitou Springs, a town close to the base of Pikes Peak, to scarf down some grub. Manitou Springs is where I got the buckskin fringe Billy jacket in 1973 cuz some thief ripped of my Levi jacket.

When we got to the Main Drag where the cafes were, we saw these cool old choppers parked out on the street. I was hypnotized by this Sportster Chopper back then, and quite frankly, still am today. It had a molded in gas tank like the ones I had seen in chopper magazines back then. Molding in a gas tank is a total commitment. Cuz if a mounting tab ever breaks and leaks, you are fucked cuz ya can't take that tank off. It would be massive work to fix it, ruin the molding, take off the tank and repair the leak, then how do ya mold and repaint it blending it in? Maybe ya can't? Anyhow, I never had the balls to mold in a gas tank, but this guy sure did, and he did it in spades, a perfect job.

Now somebody on the sidewalk musta told me about this bike cuz maybe I was asking questions? I dunno, but I seem to remember somebody telling us that this Chopped Sportster belongs to a local painter guy there named Spider, and he used this bike as his rolling business card for his shop which did outstanding paint work, which is just phenomenal. Check out the naked lady on top of the gas tank and that molded neck and the girder fork. This was the type of chopper that I could stand and stare at for an hour and never be bored, cuz I'd be finding something else new on it, I wish I'da gotten some close up pictures of the other bikes in the background, but I didn't. Next stop is gonna be Canon City, where the world's highest suspension bridge is.

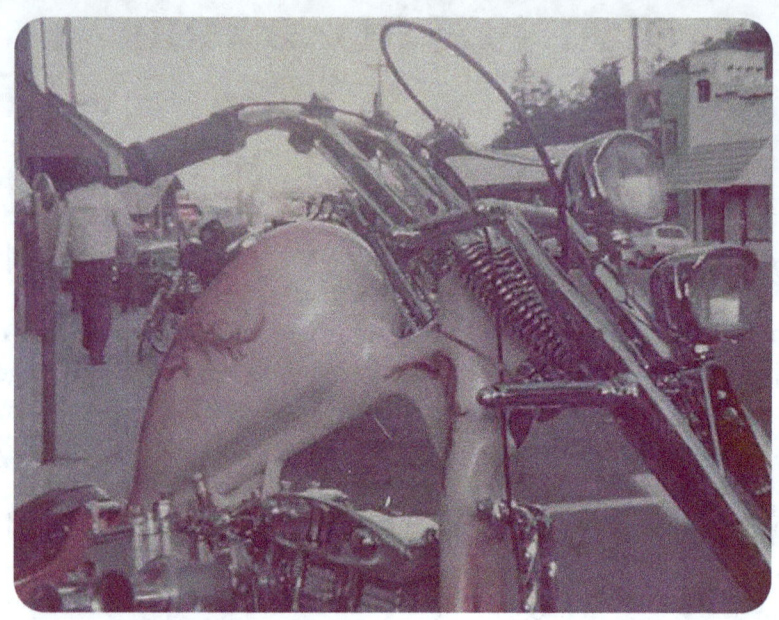

THE EARLY YEARS

THE 1975 ROAD TRIP

Part 23: "Ridin' to Canon City, Colorado"

Ridin' outta Manitou Springs, the next stop on the agenda for the Norton and two Shovelheads was Canon City. They pronounced it Can-yun City. Manitou Springs sits around 6,400 feet elevation and Canon City is 50 miles away and it's a downhill ride dropping over 1,000 feet,…down to about 5,300 feet elevation. What the hell's in Canon City? All kinds of cool stuff. There's Colorado State Pen, but we don't wanna go there, hahaha. But folks do say it's great for good camping, fishing and hiking.

The Arkansas River snakes along through the bottoms of the canyons in the mountains, and some folks like to go white water rafting on it, cuz it can be a really fast moving river at times. There's also dinosaur remains around the area and the main attraction has to be The Royal Gorge Bridge, which is supposed to be the highest suspension bridge in the world. There is a railroad that runs along the Arkansas River waaaaay down below, underneath the bridge. I understand they stopped people from driving or riding motorsickles over that bridge today. But this story ain't about today. This tale is from 1975 and we rode right acrost the sucker, hahaha.

The 1975 Road Trip

Part 24: "Ridin' Across the Royal Gorge"

The World's Highest Suspension bridge is built with a cable system like the Golden Gate Bridge. And in order to get the coupla photos of us Ridin' across the Royal Gorge my baby brudder climbs off his 71 Shovelhead and shimmied his way up the cables in the bridge's suspension. Imagine tryin' that action today? Security cameras bustin' you and the cops comin' at you from both directions all mad as hell, hahaha? But this was 1975.

So Brudder Charles risked his 18 year old life and scooted on up the bridge cables with the cheapie Kodak Instamatic camera and took this action picture of Johnny on his Snortin' Norton and me on the 74 AMF Turd, ridin' acrost the wooden planked bridge. And yes, you could ride your motorsickle along the bridge and look through the cracks between the planks and see the river and railroad tracks over 1,000 feet below. The other photo is our three steeds resting on the rim of the canyon before we took off again.

THE EARLY YEARS

The 1975 Road Trip

Part 25: "Buckskin Joe's"

So once you are at the Royal Gorge Bridge, ya kick over your motorsickle and it's just a quick 10 minute ride to Buckskin Joe's. What is a Buckskin Joe's? It's a really cool old cowboy town out there in the middle of nowhere next to the gorge and the railroad. It's sort of a real town but also a fake set up. The buildings were all real, they were old timey structures built in the 1800s from all around the state of Colorado.

Then in 1957 Metro-Goldwyn-Mayer went around the state and bought up the old original cowboy-time buildings and brought them to Buckskin Joe's to make a western town film set. And they had a donkey for a mayor, and the donkey had free run of the town, hahaha. John Wayne's movies "True Grit" and "The Cowboys" were filmed there, along with "Cat Ballou" and several other western movies and TV shows.

While we were there they had a cowboy shoot out in the dirt street and they had hung a poor guy over by Boot Hill. The town had a saloon and general store, livery stable and some other western town memorabilia like that. In these photos we have a Last Chance Saloon gal welcoming us in from the heat, the Sackett House Hotel, a dead guy on a hangman's rope and of course,... Boot Hill.

THE EARLY YEARS

SHOVELHEAD DAVE

The 1975 Road Trip

Part 26: "Flat-Coast-Spit-Fight"

After the Canon City excitement was over and done with, we loaded up the back packs on the three motorsickles and took off headed north toward Wyoming. At the beginning of this road trip, we had planned on ridin' to Yellowstone to see Old Faithful and the Grand Teton Mountain Range. But first we gotta get through Colorado. And we had some obstacles in the way.

The first obstacle happened when we came out of a cafe from eatin' lunch. The three bikes were just sittin' there doin' nuthin' but the bottom of Charles' front tire was flat. Hmm. That probably ain't good. But luckily we had some of that kinda new-fangled stuff in the can called Fix A Flat with us and that stuff got the front tire aired back up, and it held until we got to a Harley dealer to fix the flat correctly. Charles' 71 Shovel needed a new tube and one of the mechanics on duty jumped right in on it.

And after he got the flat fixed, he asked Charles if the bike had been vibratin' much? Charles said no more than usual, and after all, he'd only had it for a month or so. Turns out there was no bolt in the top motor mount. The mechanic said he put one in and from then on, Charles said it rode better with less vibration. So that was Obstacle #1 fixed.

Obstacle #2 was involving some fun. When we got up in the high country, we'd get to the sign announcing whatever summit elevation or top of the pass we were at. Then we'd wait until there were no 18 wheelers or other car traffic coming up from behind us, and we'd line up the Snortin' Norton and the 2 Shovelheads three abreast across the lane on top of the summit. Motors were off. We're just sittin' there on dead bikes.

There was only one rule in the Coast Race. You got just one push with both your feet, that was it. So we'd yell "ready,…set,… GO!" And all three of us would do the One Big Push with both feet, then we'd bring our feet up onto the foot pegs, lay down on the gas tanks like we're doin' a hunnerd, and off we'd go on the Downhill Coast Race. We'd be yellin' and laughin' and zig zaggin' the bikes back and forth doing 2 mph, then we'd get up to 15 or 20 mph, next thing ya know we'd be doin' 55 or 60, then maybe up to 80 or so, coasting on dead bikes down the back sides of the high mountain passes, hahaha. And the speed limit back then was only 55, so we were breaking the law and we won.

It was really fun racin' along with no motor noise. All we'd hear was the wind going by us and our tires on the pavement and the chains whirlin' around the sprockets. Dang, I'm laughing about it right now typing this story out, hahaha. So that's why we didn't make a lot of good time up in the Colorado High Country, cuz we were busy having fun instead of worrying about how many miles we were gettin' in that day. That was Obstacle #2.

Now for Obstacle #3. The Spit Fights. If you are of the squeamish variety, you can skip this part and go to the next chapter. And if you are still reading this, well then, you have been warned. Ya see, my Baby Brudder and me liked bitin' and spittin' ever since we wuz little kids. Don't ask me why, cuz I dunno. Maybe it was from watching rasslin' on TV, when the rasslers would knock the crap outta each other with a fantastic haymaker, and we'd see a big wad of spit go flyin' through the air. And we liked how they'd bite each other, like Mad Dog Vachon loved to do,…even though it was an illegal move, hah.

Anyhow, from our little kid tricycle days to our early teenager bicycle days to our late teenager motorsickle days, we had Spit Fights out on the highways.

Now there is also only One Rule in the Spit Fights. You spit, that's it. And it could happen at any time. The three of us could be puttin' along enjoying the nice scenery, say Johnny and me ridin' up

THE EARLY YEARS

front with Charles in the back, and suddenly Charles would come zoomin' around me on my left, cut back in front, and then he'd spit a big gob really quick and it was my job to dodge it, and if I didn't,... well,...you know. I'd get a face full of spit. Gross, eh? So we'd also do Spit Fights through the mountains. I don't think Cuzzin Johnny was involved with the Spit Fights very much cuz we liked him pretty good.

But one time in Marietta Oklahoma, still in 1975, Charles and me rode the Shovels up and met Johnny at the Little Brownie Cookie Shop and we each got a bag of those cookies shaped like windmills, and we had Windmill Cookie Fights ridin' the motorsickles up the highway to Ardmore, throwing cookies back and forth at each other, so that was kinda close to Spit Fights. And hey, the roads can be sorta flat and straight out there, you can get kinda bored at times, so gimme a break, hahaha.

Here's some pictures, one of Colorado High Country where we had the Coast Races and Spit Fights, and three pictures of Charles and me in the beginning and the middle of our bitin' and Spit Fight Years and one photo is of us teenagers tearing up what's left of a 1925 Chrysler. Next up is the Wyoming border coming at us.

The 1975 Road Trip

Part 27: "Big Wonderful Wyoming"

After the minor flat tire breakdown with the lost motor mount bolt and the quiet and funny coast races with the nasty spit fights, we headed on up north to Wyoming. I guess ya might say we had kind of a lackadaisical plan as to where we were headed. We had talked about trying to make it to Canada like our Cuzzin Paul and I had done two years earlier in 1973, and we had also talked about going to see Old Faithful, the stinky buffaloes, Snake River, and the Grand Tetons, cuz the Tetons gotta be one of the most interesting mountain ranges in this country. I always liked how spiked and jagged their snow capped peaks were, like a Stegosaurus dinosaur backbone. And Snake River was kind of an added famous attraction, cuz just the year before in 1974 Evel Knievel did his jump at Twin Falls across the Snake River Canyon, if you are old enough to remember that dare devil action.

Anyhow, when we got into Wyoming, we pulled over to take this photo of our three iron horses with the billboard horse right here. You can tell from lookin' at it that this border sign ain't exactly out on the safe straight and narrow part of the highway. It is on a slight hill and the highway goes curving around the corner. After we took the photo and stretched our legs a bit, we climbed back on the bikes to take off. And just as Cuzzin Johnny was starting out on his Snortin' Norton, here comes this station wagon (remember them things?) blastin' around the corner and nearly wiped him out. So, we were kinda nervous taking off again.

As we rode on into Wyoming, we eventually had to get gas and stuff our bellies, so we pulled into a truck stop on the highway. And it was there at the truck stop that we got warned of what was up ahead. The truckers and some of the touristy type folks who had just come down from the way we were headed told us about some huge ass snow storms that had closed down Yellowstone. Well,…shit. If that don't tear the rag off the bush, eh? There went that plan. Now we ain't a-gonna be ridin' our motorsickles to Yellowstone. So we decided to take Plan B, which was a big left turn and head west to Utah, cuz Utah also has some nice big ass mountains to ride through.

THE 1975 ROAD TRIP

Part 28: "Headed to Utah"

After finding out Yellowstone was snowed in and that mean ol' south bound snow storm was headed toward us tryin' to ruin our Plan A Road Trip destination, our little trio of motorsickles turned left and headed out I-80 west to Utah, cuz they got lots of incredibly nice mountains to ride 'sickles through as well.

Utah has the Rockies in the northern part of the state and the highest mountains they have are the Uinita Mountains, which run east to west instead of north to south like other mountain ranges, kinda weird, eh? Then there's the Wellsville Mountains, the Wah Wah Mountains, La Sal Mountains, Mineral Mountains, and then there's all the plateaus and fancy rock formations and caves. So it seemed like a good destination for an alternate Plan B Road Trip.

As we kept ridin' west on I-80 tryin' desperately to get outta Wyoming, it seemed like the storm was after us. I do not remember having any snowflakes or drizzly rain, but I do remember how cold it got and I remember how the sky was turning dark in the middle of the day. Yikes.

When you're out there on two wheels in the middle of nowhere, the weather can play a major part in your daily life, right? So we kept on haulin' ass toward Utah. Out by Fort Bridger Wyoming, just before the border, you run into the rivers like the Muddy River and the Little Muddy and then you go into the Uinita Range. The elevation out in this area is around 6,500 to 7,000 feet, so we were up pretty high,…and cold.

And while Cuzzin Johnny and Brudder Charles were smart and were wearing their big heavy wooly fleece lined jackets, all I had on was my light weight Easy Rider movie Billy Fringe Jacket, hahaha. There ain't no lining in it, only 3 buttons on front and the sleeves were open at the end and sucked cold wind up inside just fine. This was not much fun, lemme tell ya. And this ass freezin' experience is what got me to finally spend the bucks and get that nice warm 1975 AMF Black Leather Jacket immediately after this trip.

We rode through the bigger town in that area of far western Wyoming, called Evanston, which sits at 6,748 feet. Then we finally crossed the Utah border and that's where this photo is from. Johnny's Snortin' Norton seat is empty, so that means he took this photo of frozen Charles and me, and you can see how the sky ain't lookin' none too friendly for some motorsickle folks out sightseeing. And somehow, we seem to have our jean jackets over our big ones? Hmm. After Cuzzin Johnny took this picture, we rode on westward toward Salt Lake City. If it gets any warmer, we might even get to swim and float in the Great Salt Lake while we are in Utah, who knows? And then?

THE EARLY YEARS

The temperature kept dropping so we got the Norton Commando and the two Shovelheads closer together in a tight formation like a swarm of angry bumble bees and we started drafting an 18-wheeler who was making some pretty good time. That's a nice way to say we were tail-gating a semi-truck who mighta been speeding just a tad.

And of course, next thing ya know, there's the fockin' red lights flashing behind us. We got pulled over by a Utah State Trooper. But he turned out to be a nice guy. He told us he got a call from the trucker on his CB Radio and the trucker had asked the trooper to pull us over and tell us to get off his tail-gate cuz he couldn't see us back there and didn't want us dead. The trooper also told us that the trucker had asked him to not give us tickets. The trucker said he rode bikes too, and he knew what we were doing,…just tryin' to stay warm. So the nice trooper let us go. Wow.

So what did we do next? We started up them three scooters, pulled out onto I-80, got up to speed, and then we got up behind another 18-wheeler tryin' to stay warm, hahaha. I know most people reading this have probably done the same thing. When it is cold, you can draft those semis and it's like you are riding in a little vacuum. The truck kinda sucks you along with it and as long as it ain't rainin', you can stay warmer that way. Charles was on the left hand side of our lane, Cuzzin Johnny was behind Brudder Charles, and I was over on the right hand side of the lane. Charles and me were just a few feet off the semi's back door and we're probably doin' around 60 or so. And then?

And then we got this funny smell really quick, and then… POW! WHOOOSH!

A smoky explosion went off right in front of us, the right rear tire on the semi blew! I ducked down as quick as a cat can lick its butt with its tail up and its tongue out. I sucked my chest down onto the gas tank so fast and hard it nearly blew my eyes out, hahaha, cuz that big ass chunk of tire rubber came flying right over the top of me where my head had been. Whew! Close call…

So we didn't tail-gate the semis any more after that escapade, hahaha. I know some people may say we were lucky to not get hit by the tire tread, and some just file it away and say shit can happen, but I think what happened was this,...the Mormon God up on the Planet/Star Kolob was trying to kill me. I got no idea how many times since 1973 I have been out on two wheeled adventures riding cross country and had some bitter angry gods up in the heavens get mad at me for no apparent reason and try to kill me off.

But,...they have all missed,...so far.

THE 1975 ROAD TRIP

Part 29: "Invading Salt Lake City"

After freezin' our butts off ridin' out in the majestic mountains in western Wyoming and northeastern Utah, we zigged and zagged a bit on the Utah highways until we made it into Salt Lake City, which sits up a little over 4,200 feet elevation. After camping out a bit and stayin' at a coupla roadside motels along the way, this time we were gonna be High Rollers. We rode them motorsickles right smack dab into the middle of downtown Salt Lake City and got us a big ol' room at the Hotel Utah, one of the fanciest joints in the city.

We soon discovered $$$ that the Hotel Utah was THE top rated hotel in Salt Lake City and certainly in the rest of the state. It was a beautiful old building, built in 1911, right on the corner of Main Street and South Temple, in the heart of downtown. It had a Grande lobby, a really fancy reception desk and killer restaurant with great food.

And,…they didn't like us one bit, to them, we were just three
   oversize scruffy road bums coming in stinkin' of diesel fuel and regular road exhaust, all windblown, looking like bums that just crawled outta the dumpster in their back alley. And I guess we were. But,…we had cash, and cash is king.

We left the Norton and two Shovelhead motorsickles down in their parking garage, unpacked our bikes, threw the road gear over our shoulders and moseyed in through the door as if we were normal people, then we went traipsing right through their glorious lobby with our grimy road gear, tents and sleeping bags, hahaha. The peoples' reactions were kinda like we just landed from Outer Space.

While I do have a few photos of the inside of the Hotel Utah, sadly, I ain't got no photos of the magnificent outside of it. And the Mormons later ruined it by turning it into a museum, so it ain't a hotel no more. So this photo here is of one of their other nice Mormon buildings close by, which we toured the next day. And the longer we stayed here in Salt Lake City, which was two whole days,… the more they seemed to dislike us. I wonder why?

The 1975 Road Trip

Part 30: "Havin' Fun in Salt Lake City"

The next morning, we three motorsickle folks woke up fairly well rested from sleeping on actual nice comfy hotel beds instead of wakin' up in sleeping bags in our pup tents on the hard bumpy ground, hahaha. We got all clean, even put on some clean clothes for a change, and got into their old timey elevator and started down to the lobby for some breakfast. For some reason beyond me now, we wanted to see how tough the old elevator was, so we three Cuzzins who were over 200- pounders each, started jumpin' up and down in that elevator for a torture test, and…it failed and broke. It shut down and that damn thing left us stranded between floors. So we had to pry the nice old elevator doors open while we were in between floors, and luckily, the floor was only about 3 feet up from where the door opened, so we climbed up and out onto that floor then had to walk down the stairs and told the guys at the reception desk that the dang elevator was busted.

We ate breakfast in the hotel, then walked over a coupla streets and took a Mormon Tour. Now there are buildings the Mormons keep open to tourists, like anybody can go in. Then there are buildings that only Mormons can enter, and last but not least, there are places that only the highest-ranking Mormons can enter, even the regular sinful Mormons hafta stay out.

So we went into a regular building for the tour, and the tour guide told us all about Joseph Smith and how the Angel Moroni came down from Mormon Heaven and told Joseph Smith about the Golden Plates that were buried in a stone box. Then the tour guide told us how Smith took his hat and Magic Seer Stones and interpreted the writings, blah, blah, blah, you know the drill. So when that section of the tour was ending, the guide asked if anyone had any questions. Hmm. I raised my hand. He looked at me kinda suspiciously and said "yes?"

I said "I'd like to see those Golden Tablets, are they around here somewhere?" The guide looked kinda disgusted and said "No, the Angel Moroni took them back to Heaven with him." So I mumbled out kinda loud,… "That's a likely story." The crowd of Mormons did not find the humor in that comment. After all, they were here for some serious shit, not to hear my Texas buffoonery, hahaha. But hey, I gave 'em some cheap comedy for free, didn't even cost 'em a nickel.

Next, we went over to another beautiful building the Salt Lake Tabernacle, where the World's Largest Pipe Organ is. This is the elegant building where the Mormon Tabernacle Choir sings. Now as a 20 year old 2nd year carpenter apprentice, I was awed by this building, from its outstanding design to the incredible way they built it. The tour guide guy up at the podium had no microphone. He could whisper and we could hear him, maybe 100 feet back to where we three 'sickle guys were sitting in the rear of the auditorium.

The guide said this building is one of the most acoustically perfect structures in America, and I believe him. The guide pulled out a little straight pin, the kind your grandma sewed with, and he dropped it on his podium and we could hear it "click" when it landed. Amazing. He also told us how the pews in the building were fashioned from solid oak, hewn from one piece oak trunks from the big trees, no joints in the pews, just solid carved wood. That is a lotta work. Then he told us how the building was built with no nails or screws, just fitted wood joints. Also amazing. And then?

And then the regular tour guide guy stepped aside and the organ player guru came out, sat down at the World's Largest Pipe Organ and started playing some kinda Bach or Beethoven stuff. When they talk about a huge pipe organ, this one is it. It had small gold pipes as little as a straw in your cup up to gold pipes larger than telephone poles. It shook the windows, walls and floor when he got going good. As exciting as this was, apparently it was kinda boring to Brudder Charles, cuz he suddenly cupped his hands up to his face and yelled out "PLAY GREEN ONIONS! PLAY GREEN ONIONS!" Bwahaha! (For you younger folks, that's an old 1962 organ/instrumental rock & roll song from Booker T and the MGs.)

So the Mormon heads snapped around to see who would actually defile the sanctity of this precious moment, and,…you guessed it, it was us motorsickle bums,…again. So, we got up and scurried out the back door like some sewer rats who had hungry alley cats chasin' them, and went off to the next building where there were some statues and other nice shit like that. It's not that I am a natural born ham, but I was gonna try to be almost as annoying here in Salt Lake City as the Mormons were to us back in Dallas. Why not?

The Mormons were always leaving their little religious cards on your car, bothering you in the airports, stores and parking lots, knocking on your front door, so now it's Payback Time. Brudder Charles became the photographer and I volunteered to be the Annoying Guy. We got here a nice shot looking at their beautiful building interior, then there's me riding one of their Magic Lions out front, then another one where I'm acting like Moe from the Three Stooges yanking on Brigham Young's nose, then I stared at this other statue until I made him blink, wink, wink.

SHOVELHEAD DAVE

THE EARLY YEARS

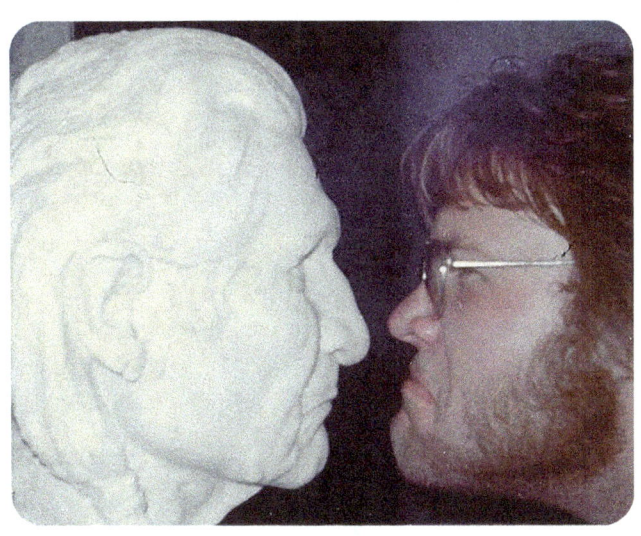

THE 1975 ROAD TRIP

Part 31: "Still in Salt Lake City"

We stayed at the Hotel Utah for a grand total of two nights,…$$$. That was it. But before we hit the road again, we took a few more photos of the shenanigans in the hotel.

This group of pictures here has another view of one of the Mormon's awesome buildings. Then there is a photo Brudder Charles took of my dumb ass winning their Hotel Utah Bubble Gum Chewing Contest, and don't ask me how or why I entered it, I have no idea. Maybe my devilish brudder or cuzzin dared me and tricked me into it? Anyhow, my big mouth won it, and there is the guy presenting the Award to me with Cuzzin Johnny looking on in support of my sore jaws, which would stay sore and have trouble chewing for a coupla days longer.

THE EARLY YEARS

Then Cuzzin Johnny took a coupla pictures of Charles and me sittin' on a fancy velvet covered bench in the Hotel Utah lobby, and one leaning up against the guard rail where we are being snobs like the Mormons were to us. And now it's time to pack up our bags of shit, load 'em on the Norton and the two Shovelheads and get the hell outta Salt Lake City. Next stop? Las Vegas.

The 1975 Road Trip

Part 32: "Ridin' to Las Vegas"

We packed all our road gear on the three motorsickles and got ready to leave Mormonville, aka Salt Lake City. It was fun while it lasted, but no sense in wearin' out our welcome, right? Besides, we thought it might be best to leave on our own accord before they tarred and feathered us and locked us up in those wooden stocks the Pilgrims used where they lock your hands and feet in the holes so the Mormon kids could come by and poke us with sharp pointy sticks and other goofy shit like that. This is supposed to be our vacation and our fun time, not theirs. Right? Right.

Going off our road map, it looked like we had a bit over 400 miles to ride to get to Las Vegas, which back then was a full day's ride at the 55 mph speed limit. We'd already had one encounter with the highway cops on this road trip, didn't want another one, hahaha. So we took off down I-15 and rode through Provo and Nephi and kept going on down south in the state. And lemme tell ya one thing, just because we left Salt Lake City doesn't mean we left the Mormon area, cuz they have the entire state. And although we were on stock bikes and looked fairly normal, we still got some stares that could freeze hot coffee solid.

In my later long haired and bearded years riding in the western states cross country on the 74 AMF Chopper, I made sure to stay outta Utah, just in case, hah. Ridin' I-15 South, you go through Fishlake National Forest where the elevation is 8,800 feet, then you go by the Black Rock desert. which I'd hate to cross in a covered wagon like the pioneers did,...and then you ride along next to the Mineral Mountains. By the time you ride down by the Cedar City

THE EARLY YEARS

area, you are at 5,800 feet, so even down in their 'lower land' they still sit as high as Denver. Hmm.

The last two towns we rode through in Utah were Washington and St. George. Then we putted right through the very top northwest corner of Arizona for about 35 miles, then I-15 quickly got us into the bottom southeast corner of Nevada, and that's where we stopped and took this fuzzy picture. We now had a little less than 100 miles to get to Las Vegas. Yay!

THE 1975 ROAD TRIP

Part 33: "Ridin' into Las Vegas"

This nice clear photo is off an old post card we got in Las Vegas, not from the Kodak Instamatic, hahaha. We rode into Las Vegas before sunset and since we were now in the desert, that means we were no longer freezin' our butts off up in the mountains like the previous few days. We got back to ridin' in T shirts, which was nice.

Once we got into the city, we rode up and down The Strip taking in the sights. We went over by the Horseshoe where they had the million bucks on display, rode by the Golden Nugget, the Dunes, the Flamingo, Sahara, Frontier, and the cool one with the huge neon cowboy, the Pioneer Club. Man, that was some sight for us travelin' motorsickle kids from Texas and Oklahoma.

We pulled the three road weary hot motorsickles into the Stardust. We left the three bikes outside to cool off and fend for themselves and then we headed on up into the casino to see the sights and have some fun. We'd heard about how good the steak dinners were in Las Vegas and we were itchin' to chomp on some of those that night for dinner.

We shoulda stayed in our room and gotten clean first and then went out to have some fun, but instead, all those flashing lights and bells going off downstairs had kinda hypnotized us. So we dropped all our road gear stuff on the floor in the room, jumped in an elevator and headed on down to see what the gamblin' action was all about. None of us had ever done it, of course. All we'd seen of sinful gamblin' was the cowboys on western TV shows and the gangsters in movies having fun playing cards and roulette, maybe shootin' each other once in a while. Now we were gonna try it, cuz winning lots of money looked like lots of easy fun,...right?

Charles and Johnny headed off with their loot to the slot machines, and this was back when they paid out in silver dollars and had the handles on the sides you'd pull, not the boring kind they have today where you push the electronic button and sit there bored and the thing tells you that you just lost. The old timey slots were a blast, exciting to play, even if ya lost. Meanwhile, I was meandering around looking at everything else, just taking it all in. Then,... I spied this big shiny and glittery sparkly wheel on the wall.

They called it the Stardust/Lido Wheel, if I remember right. It was mesmerizing. It was a big wheel up on the wall. It was like a spoked wagon wheel, and out on the edges were the spaces showing the money to bet and win. So half the spots on the edges were one dollar bills, then half of the spaces left were two dollar bills, then a smaller segment was five dollar bills, then even smaller for the tens, a few spots had the twenties, then there was only one slot that said Stardust and one slot that said Lido. And the Stardust and Lido spots paid out 40 to 1.

They had this really beautiful saloon type gal spinning the wheel, and she was wearing the skimpiest of Las Vegas show girl costumes. She had these big breats-ses,...two of 'em,...and they would jiggle when she spun the wheel. And I ain't jokin'. She seemed as nice as Miss Kitty on Gunsmoke, maybe even nicer. So I moseyed up to the table and got me some chips and started puttin' them on the spots in front of me. I started out cautiously, so as to get kinda used to it. I put some chips on the 1, the 2, and 5 spots.

The Purdy Lady with the two big breasts-ses spun the wheel, and it landed on my 5 spot. So the nice guy that worked the table took his nice stick with the nice hook on the end and he slid me 5 more chips, but he took away the ones I had on the 1 and 2 spots. Big deal, I'm still ahead. I kept playin' and I kept winnin'. I am thinking to myself,...man, whoever the guy was that invented this free money wheel is probably dead out in the desert by a cactus bush, or maybe he's dead at the bottom of a lake wearing cement boots, cuz this money wheel is sooo fuckin' easy, it just gives you money for free. What goofy bozo came up with this invention? Hahaha!

So this action kept going for maybe 45 minutes or an hour, and by that time I had gathered up the courage to start bettin' big, like a real high roller on TV, hahaha. I even started betting on the Stardust and Lido spots and guess what? They hit. That's right. So the Purdy Lady would jiggle her boobs and shake her butt and spin the wheel, and she made it stop where I wanted it to, then the Nice Stick Guy would push more chips over to my pile with his stick that had the nice hook on the end. And my job was to take all the chips he pushed over to me and make nice stacks of them right in front of me, like I'd seen Maverick do on TV. Things were going just fine and dandy. And then?

And then Brudder Charles and Cuzzin Johnny came moseyin' back over to where I was, and they had those Sad Hound Dog Looks on their faces, and they told me how them greedy One Armed Bandits had cleaned them out. They were now broke. They were all gloomy. So they see me all happy and smilin'. They wondered what was up. Then I pointed down to the table and they saw the big ass pile of stacked chips in front of me and they asked "Is all of that yours?" I said "Yep, and don't worry about what ya'll lost, it don't matter now, and we are gonna be eatin' high on the hog tonight. We are gonna have the biggest thickest juiciest steaks this place has."

They both got all excited at our new free wealth and they said they were going up to our room to get cleaned up and get ready for the fun night at the Stardust in Las Vegas,…yay! Sounds good, right? And it coulda been good and it woulda been good and it shoulda been good, if'n only I'da been smart and left with them to head up to the room. I coulda been a hero. I probably had four to five hunnerd bucks right there in front of me, all I had to do was cash out.

We coulda had a fun and successful leisurely ride back home, eating all the best food, riding on Route 66 taking our time, stopping at fancy road side motels with swimming pools, THAT is what shoulda happened. And the winnings from that free money wheel woulda paid for it all. But that's not what happened. Instead, I ended up being a zero. So now this 1975 Road Trip story takes a different turn for its brutal ending. Sigh…

That fockin' bitch at the free money wheel started making it land on all the other peoples' numbers, dammit. And that greedy fucker with his gawddamn hooked stick started yanking my hard earned piles of chips away. And within an hour or so, it was all gone. GONE! So now I'm standin' there,…still in my filthy road clothes, all grimy and nasty and flat ass broke,…and here comes Brudder Charles and Cuzzin Johnny all happy bouncin' down the stairs, both nice and clean in their clean jeans and t shirts, and they are much-o hon-gry and ready for their steak dinners. Gulp. Oooops.

The 1975 Road Trip

Part 34: "Stardust"

This 'borrowed' beautiful picture of the now-defunct and sadly imploded Stardust obviously did not come from my cheapie Kodak Instamatic camera, cuz there is no way it could ever take a photo this nice at night. This photo is from a post card.

So on that Fateful Stardust Magic Night, I'm standing there at the Stardust/Lido Free Money Wheel and now I'm flat broke while Brudder Charles and Cuzzin Johnny thought I had all the winnings and we had it made. But,… I blew it. We had to go back to the room and figure out a Plan A. Back up in the room, we discovered what a dire situation we were in.

And when I say we were flat broke, I don't mean we were down to maybe 15 or 20 bucks each, I mean when we emptied out all our pockets on one of the beds we didn't even have 5 lousy bucks combined. That's how broke we were. In Las Vegas,…well over 1,000 miles from home. We went to sleep that night very hon-gry with no din-din.

Next morning? OK, now what the hell are we gonna do,… besides not have any breakfast cuz we're broke? First off, Charles is 18 and Johnny is 19 and while I'm a 20 year old home owner, I ain't got no BankAmeriCard or Master Charge. To you younger folks, that's what they call your Visa and Mastercard today. So we ain't got no cash and we ain't got no credit card.

First up, some of you might think for Plan A, 'go call your folks and tell them you need some money.' No way, Jose. Our folks are all tea totallin' anti-gamblin' anti-drinkin' hard shell (as our mom liked to say) Southern Baptists. There is no way in hell I am about to call the folks and tell them what we did. I mean, OK, I'm out on my own already, but Little Brudder Charles is still 18, just got outta high school a coupla weeks ago, and if the folks find out what happened, Charles might get grounded, bwahahaha! As for what Cuzzin Johnny's folks would do? Unmentionable terrors could await him as well.

OK so here comes Plan B. I always carried an old folded up blank check in my wallet for emergencies. Well if this ain't an emergency I don't know what is. Yeah! The emergency check, that's it! We went down to the reception desk counter where we had checked in the day before and told them we needed to cash a check. I told the guy I'm from Dallas and handed him my driver's license for proof of ID to match the name on the check and I asked if I could write him this check for 100 bucks.

He laughed at me. He said the Stardust is a casino, not a bank and they do not cash peoples' checks, especially out of state checks. Hmm. Rat farts. I asked him who does. He told us about a coupla places down the street that cash outta state checks. OK, that is our new Plan C. We went down the street to the address of the place he told us about. What a grimy dump. It looked like a scene outta some old black and white 1950s film noir movie. Two goons sitting at two cheap metal desks in the back of the room, cigarette smoke thick in the air like my favorite pool hall back home, and there's only two of them in the joint?

I explained Plan C to the film noir guys. Told them I needed to write them a check for 100 bucks, could they cash one from Dallas? They said sure, they can do it. But if I want a 100 bucks to take with us, I need to write it for 125 bucks, cuz they charge 25 bucks to cash it. What the fuck? Really? They said if I write one for 100 bucks I can only get 75 from them. Shit, and double shit. And now I ain't sayin' nuthin' for certain right here, but there is a distinct possibility that these two guys may or may not have had a little somethin'-somethin' to do with a certain organization which may or may not have somethin' to do with running a certain place called Las Vegas. So we left the clip joint.

Plan D is to go to the other check cashing joint, maybe they have better rates, hahaha? When we walked into the same kinda dump, same action. Same 25 bucks fee to cash the check for 100. And here's the deal,...when I was packing up to leave on

this road trip, I took all the cash outta my checking account except for 120 bucks that I left in there to cover the next house payment, which was 104 bucks that was due in a few days. I'm stymied. And no, I ain't got no savings account, cuz I ride a 1974 AMF Strike Made Shovelhead that keeps me broke, hahaha. Desperation set in.

Plan E is to go to a regular bank. So we did. Guy at the bank sez they do not cash checks from out of staters cuz they got burned on too many bounced checks, so no dice at the bank. And when the bank guy looked at my Texas driver's license, he kinda scowled and said "You boys shouldn't be gambling anyhow." At first, I thought he was giving us some unasked for advice, kinda like bossy step father to illegitimate stepson crap, but when we walked out the door to the bikes, it dawned on us that we were underage and it was illegal for folks under 21 to gamble, hahaha. Should we go back to the Stardust and demand all our lost loot back? Did we wanna end up

THE EARLY YEARS

with cement boots down in the bottom of the lake? Not really. So we departed that place and now the desperation left and raw panic has set in.

Enter Plan F: Next we went to a phone booth,…who remembers them things? I put the coins in the slots to make the call, dialed the number with a real dial and was hoping I would not get put on hold, cuz we didn't have many coins left. I pulled the old blank check outta my wallet so I'd know the account number and asked to talk to the guy who set up my house payments, and he's the guy who did our folks' mortgage back in 1949, so this guy is a family friend that has known our folks longer than we have known them. Mister Sutton at my State Bank is our last hope now. I told him what was up. He also went to the same Baptist Church our folks went to. Gulp. Is he gonna rat us out? He could not believe we were gambling and went broke in Vegas, hahaha. I told him how we had been on a cross country motorcycle trip and just happened to be riding through Las Vegas when we ran outta money. He bit.

Now this bank is also the bank I went inside every Friday afternoon to cash my carpenter apprentice paycheck, back when they gave you paper paychecks, and Mister Sutton knows I have a house payment of $104 due in a few days and he sees I only got 120 bucks in my account,…gulp. He also knows when a carpenter ain't working, the carpenter ain't gettin' paid,…another gulp. I told him I had just finished the job at Six Flags Over Texas, got laid off, took this road trip for Charles' high school graduation present, and reminded Mister Sutton that I'd have an unemployment check waiting for me in the mailbox when I got back home and that check would cover the house payment. Triple gulp. He bit again.

So Mister Sutton was kind enough to wire us the 100 bucks through Western Union. YAY! So now we're gettin' 100 measly bucks to split among the three of us, and we gotta ride 1,200 miles back home,…through the desert. And that is supposed to be good?

The 1975 Road Trip

Part 35: "Gettin' the Hell Outta Vegas!"

Once the 100 bucks got to us in Las Vegas from the electronic wire transfer sent from my now empty checking account back in Dallas, I got it split into 10 ten dollar bills. By this time in the day Brudder Charles, Cuzzin Johnny and me hadn't ate in a looong time. We missed the steak dinner that vanished into the Free Money Wheel and never happened the night before, then no breakfast and lunch so far today. But that was about to change right then and there, hahaha. We wuz hungry.

But here's the sad part, for me, anyhow. We had to go to a fockin' McDonalds for some burgers. Four years earlier in 1971, I had been a 16 year old punk kid flippin' burgers at Jack in the Box, and McDonald's was our sworn enemy, our main competition. So for me to hafta go get burgers from those asshole McDonalds guys was kinda like rubbin' extra salt in my Jack in the Box burger patties, hahaha. I always took that Jack in the Box job seriously, cuz that is the job that got me the paychecks to help get the old used 1967 Sportster,…see? And to this day, I still proudly fly my old 1971 'Jack in the Box' patch on my Levi cut off, so there!

OK, now back to the action, folks. Charles told me years later that he still remembers when I walked outta that McDonalds with the bag of three burgers,…not the 6 or 9 burgers which we wanted. Charles said as I handed them the burgers, "Enjoy 'em fellas, cuz it might be the last thing we get to eat until we get back home."

So we wolfed down them little burgers and got ready to hit the road and get the hell outta Las Vegas. I then gave Cuzzin Johnny 3 of the 10 dollar bills, then gave 3 of 'em to Charles, and kept the last

THE EARLY YEARS

3 for me. That's all the bucks we have now. 30 bucks each to make it over 1,200 miles through the desert. Nice thought, eh?

We already had the bikes loaded up ready to go. So after we et, Cuzzin Johnny kicked over his Norton Commando cuz it was kick start only, I kicked over my 74 AMF Shitbike cuz the electric starter never worked anyhow, and Brudder Charles pushed the starter button on his 71 FL cuz it never had a kicker to begin with, and just like that,…we're off. OK now here's a picture of my Levi cut off with the Jack in the Box patch, just in case anyone thought I was bullshittin'. And that's it right above the Texas Flag patch.

THE 1975 ROAD TRIP

Part 36: "Back on the Road"

After scarfin' down the McDonalds hamburgers in Las Vegas around noon, the bikes were packed up with our road gear and we hit the road again, headed southeast out toward the big Hoover Dam which was only about 30 minutes or so away. After we rode over the Hoover, we got up on the other side and Cuzzin Johnny took this photo right here. Now this photo has a funny shiny look to it on the right hand side and the reason why is cuz it's a photo of the old 1975 photo, cuz the original one is stuck in my old photo album like glue, hahaha. And I ain't gonna ruin the original by pulling it out to take a scan of it and take a chance on it ripping it in half. So after Johnny took this photo, we rode into Arizona.

Now I wanted to make damn sure I was 100% correct before I write this next part, cuz it sounds kinda awful and maybe a little bit unbelievable, hahaha. So I asked Brudder Charles the other day,… "After we ate them burgers in Vegas before we lit outta town with our tails between our legs, do you remember eating anything,…anything at all,…before we got back home to Dallas? Do you remember eating anything even as simple as a candy bar out of a vending machine at a gas station?"

Charles said "Nope, we never ate one damn thing on the entire trip back home." And I asked Cuzzin Johnny if he remembered us eating anything at all on the trip between Las Vegas and home. He said no. And as for myself, I do not remember eating anything at all between Las Vegas and home, so I am going with that painful verdict. We did not eat anything on the entire 1,200+ mile ride back home, not even some Tail of Rat or Lizard Stew, cuz we were too broke. All our meager cash had to go in our gas tanks. So here we go, off into the hot ass sandy desert with empty bellies and 30 bucks each, and I had just a few extra bucks change, like maybe 7 bucks or so, from the 10 dollar bill I gave them at McDonalds for the burgers. That was it. Sigh.

The 1975 Road Trip

Part 37: "Crossin' the Desert"

After we crossed the Hoover Dam, we caught Highway 93 when we crossed the Arizona Border and we took that down to Kingman where we caught I-40 East. And as many of you know, I-40 is the same east/west direction along the old Route 66 for much of the way. So now we are riding out through the desert country. We didn't even need to look at our road map for a loooong time until we get to Amarillo, Texas, which is now 750 miles away.

From Kingman we rode east out through the Juniper Mountains and the little semi-ghost town of Seligman, which sits a little over 7,000 feet elevation. It's high desert land out that way. Then came Williams and the next town of any size after that is Flagstaff, elevation still over 6,900 feet. But it was kinda nice ridin' at this stage, no more worries about snow or cold rain, on through Winslow and Holbrook we journeyed, stopping only for gas. Next we rode through the Painted Desert and the Petrified Forest area. Chambers, Sanders, Houck and Lupton were the last four towns we rode through in Arizona.

Trivia Question: What's in Houck, Arizona?
Answer: Fort Courage, the set of the TV show "F Troop." We didn't stop to see the fort but we did see the big billboards advertising it.

Here is our Arizona Border photo, and now suddenly Cuzzin Johnny is #35."

THE EARLY YEARS

The 1975 Road Trip

Part 38: "Headin' Home"

Next we crossed into New Mexico. We didn't bother to take a photo at the New Mexico border this time cuz we already had one from riding the other way, haha. We rode through Gallup and headed on to Albuquerque. By this time we had covered almost 600 miles and were about half way home. And that means we had been in the saddle for 12 or 13 hours by now. And since we had left Vegas around noon, that means it was now around midnight out in the New Mexico desert.

I will say riding in the desert at night is a lot of fun,…if ya ain't broke and starvin' and ya hafta keep riding forever, hahaha. Lots of the cars are gone by midnight and it's mostly the 18 wheelers that remain out there with you under the moon and stars. And by 3 or 4 o'clock in the morning, even most of the 18 wheelers are smart enough to be resting somewhere. But,…not us. We kept riding,… and riding,…and riding. We were like the Energizer Bunny.

And riding in the middle of the night and wee early morning hours means you can't really see all the purdy countryside around you, so we got kinda ripped off in that department. But we had seen lots of purdy country over the previous days,…right? Luckily for us, the truck stops were open 24 hours along the highway so we could continue the madness into the early morning hours. Then we hit Tucumcari. That meant we had now covered about 750 miles in one sitting of around 16 to 17 hours. And still, we had to push on.

We crossed into the Texas Border at the little town of Glenrio. And we kept riding and riding and riding. By this time, we couldn't take it anymore. We were goin' kinda nuts, hard to keep eyes open,

THE EARLY YEARS

getting kinda dizzy, falling asleep on the three bikes. We started getting kinda wobbly out west of Amarillo and nearly ran into each other a few times. Imagine the sound of a Norton Commando and two Shovelheads blastin' down the highway all together doing 60 mph or so in a formation and we were still gettin' sleepy? By this time we had covered a little over 850 miles in around 18 hours straight and we couldn't take it anymore. It was around sunrise time by now. We had ridden all damn night and could not keep our eyes open any longer.

Just outside Amarillo we finally gave up. No money for a cheapie motel, no money for a $5.00 spot at a KOA Kampground which mighta been closed by this time anyhow, no money for nuthin',… except gas. So we pulled into one of those Road Side Rest Areas and we pulled the bikes in close to the picnic table areas. We threw our sleeping bags on the tops of three picnic tables. And if any cops were gonna bust us for "No Overnight Camping" all we had to say is 'we weren't here overnight, this is just a little morning rest, hahaha.'

So we tried to snooze there for maybe 2 hours or so, and I ain't claiming we were sleeping, cuz I kept hearing the early morning traffic and Cuzzin Johnny remembers his picnic table being the closest one to the railroad tracks when the train came through,…

BWAAAAAH!,…went the train horn, and good morning to you,

too, Mister Train Engineer and thanks for that loud horn blast to get us going again. From Amarillo, we peeled off onto Highway 287. We rode on down 287 to Wichita Falls and got gas together for one last time.

While we were getting gas, Cuzzin Johnny states rather matter of factly,… "I hate to say anything bad about ya'lls bikes, but didya notice my Norton was the only bike that didn't give any trouble?" And he was right, his Norton Commando performed flawlessly the entire trip. And he was also right cuz my 3 circuit breakers had been going in and out the entire trip. When that 74 AMF Shitbike was brand spankin' new, the Harley dealer could not figure out what was up with those 3 circuit breakers under the seat. And after my whoppin' 90 day warranty expired, it was up to me to figure that circuit breaker shit out. I musta put in 9 different ones by this time, replaced the bases, got new wiring and it STILL fucked up, hahaha. And after 11 months with that bike now, they'd still pop and leave me dead on the side of the road. Sometimes that '74 Troublehead would make it an entire day without dying. And sometimes it'd die 3 times before lunch. It had a ghost.

And Charles' 71 had a few issues. Anybody can get a flat tire anytime, anywhere, so I'll give him a pass on that one. But his 71 lost its top motor mount bolt and had one little leaky pushrod gasket. And it was there that Charles and I split with Cuzzin Johnny,… sniff, sniff. Johnny had to take off east headed back to Ardmore Oklahoma, so he still had about 100 more miles to go than we did. Charles and me gave Johnny what little cash we had left, probably less than 7 bucks by then. We had full tanks now and were close to home, maybe 3 hours to go.

It was very sad feelin' and kinda eerie ridin' along without Cuzzin Johnny. You get used to being with folks out on the road. You get used to seeing them and hearing their motorsickles. Our three bikes had been together out on the highways for several days and we were used to hearing our exhausts blended together. Now the exhaust music had changed.

And as strange as it was for Charles and me to not hear Johnny's Norton, he had to ride on along now just by himself. While Johnny disappeared off his exit ramp headed back to his place, Charles and me made it another 3 hours into the Dallas Fort Worth traffic and finally made our way back home, totally exhausted and burned out like we had never been burned out before.

Charles got back to our folks' house and got to rest. I got back to my house which was about a mile away and sure enough,…

YAY,…there was the unemployment check waitin' in the mailbox. Now although I was dirty and filthy covered in road grime including Las Vegas desert sand, I skipped out on the shower for a bit. I stuck the 74 Shovel back in my 1 car garage, grabbed the unemployment check and hopped into the 1968 Mustang and drove over to the bank to put the check in. And while I was inside the bank, I saw Mister Sutton sitting in there at this desk and I held up the check

THE EARLY YEARS

by its top two corners and I snapped it back and forth to celebrate it being there in my hand. Mister Sutton saw that while he was on the phone and he kinda laughed at me and waved his hand in the air like he was saying 'get outta here.' So now the house payment would be covered and all was good in the Emergency 100 Dollar Wire Transfer World. I put the hunnerd back in and had a few bucks pocket money to boot.

Next? I left the bank and drove straight over to a Wyatt's Cafeteria and grabbed a tray and slid it down those 3 stainless steel rails and ordered me up a big ol' crispy Chicken Fried Steak with Cream Gravy, mashed taters, fried okra, Texas Toast, and a big ass slice of that chocolate cream pie with the ants crawling on top and I et it all up with a big frosty glass of Texas Sweet Tea. Burp. And lemme tell ya, that Chicken Fried Steak tasted waaaaay better than that Las Vegas Steak we never got, bwahaha. Here is one last picture taken out in the Texas Panhandle, kinda desolate, which sums up the end of this trip.

And that, my friends, is The End of the 1975 Road Trip.

Part 39: "The Early Years"

Late Summer 1975

So, after the 1975 Spring Road Trip through the western states with Brudder Charles and Cuzzin Johnny, I did this action to the 74 AMF Shovelhead. I jacked the Super Glide up on my little homemade welded pipes lift, pulled the front wheel off, took off the fork tubes and ran them down to Shelby's Mid Cities Choppers shop where he sold me some +4 inch over tubes and I got that new seat and those handlebars from him, too. And he let me watch him do the fork tubes so I learnt right then and there on the spot how to do 'em my own damn self next time. And this photo here is in front of my little crackerbox house in Dallas Texas.

Part 40: "The Early Years"

Late Summer 1975

After the long road trip through the western states, I just rode around Texas some for the rest of the summer, taking weekend trips. I rode down to Houston, Galveston and Padre Island with my high school buddy Freddie who bought my old 67 Sportster, then I rode over to Texarkana and later down to Austin and San Marcos, but nothin' too far cuz I was working solid again,… I needed the money.

Then Brudder Charles and me decided to ride up to Oklahoma again and visit Cuzzin Johnny on his Snortin' Norton. And this time we had another friend we were raised with named Gary who was ridin' along with us on his brand new Black 1975 Sportster XLCH.

We took off up the highway to Red River and when we crossed the Red River Bridge, we were puttin' along doing maybe 65 mph or so. Charles and me were ridin' side by side up front. Charles was in the left hand side of the lane and I was over on the right hand side. And Gary was on his Black Sportster in back of us maybe 50 yards or so, or at least he WAS at the back of us.

Suddenly without any warning, here comes Gary blastin' up in my rear view mirror gettin' closer and closer, really fast, and he comes shootin' up right in between Charles and me and Gary musta been doin' 90 or 100, and he slipped in between us, but not all the way clean, cuz Gary's right side handlebar hit my left side handlebar.

The impact kinda knocked me a little bit jiggly and I heard a loud SNAP! And there went my clutch lever, I had to slam on the crappy disc brakes, turn around on the shoulder and go back looking for the end of my clutch lever,…groan. Charles and Gary came back to help in the search. Gary was kinda sheepish, apologizing and shit like that, but oh well, big deal, shit happens, right?

We finally found the end of the lever over on the shoulder. I had maybe 2 & 1/2 inches of clutch lever stub left and it was kinda hard to work it, but we managed to get the rest of the way into Ardmore Oklahoma and found a guy who welded it back together for me. Yay! What would we ever do without those Road Side Repair Guys,… right? I kept using that busted/welded aluminum clutch lever for a few more weeks until the 74 Super Glide got hacked up but good inside my little house. This here is the last photo of the Super Glide in its swing arm stage, all together. And look what great Black Mail Material this photo is with me wearin' those 1975 duds, hahaha.

Part 41: "The Early Years"

Late Summer 1975

When Charles and Gary and me rode the 'sickles into Ardmore Oklahoma, we went by Cuzzin Johnny's and found him there with his Norton ready to go. Then the four of us rode around town a bit. And too dang bad I did not have the cheapie Kodak camera with me, cuz it woulda made a nice old photo to look back at today. It woulda been like this,… Charles' Black 71 Shovel, Johnny's Black 73 Norton, my Black 74 Shovel, and Gary's Black 75 Sportster. All we needed was a Black 1972 something-or-other to complete the Flush Straight. Where were Ray and Debra on their Black 72 Super Glide when we needed them?

Then Charles and Gary and me rode back to Dallas and they went to their houses and I went to mine. Then I rode the 1974 Super Glide FXE up my plank and into the house and killed it forever. I rode it in the front door and back to its own room, then got ready to chop it all up to pieces, and yes, down on the floor there next to the tool bag, that is a picture of me riding a bull at the Kowbell Rodeo Arena in Mansfield, Texas, 1971. The custom paint on the front and rear fenders was done by another life long pal also named Gary who did it with rattle cans and masking tape in the house where it sits. Too bad this version lasted only a few weeks. And now the ultimate teardown begins.

SHOVELHEAD DAVE

PART 42: "THE EARLY YEARS"

Late Summer 1975

Well,...sigh,...now it's time to kill off that pesky irritating 1974 AMF Piece of Shit Super Glide FXE which was built right during the middle of the AMF Strike of 1974.

That fucker had humiliated and embarrassed me for the last fuckin' time. Now it is going to the firing squad, so to speak. I had fuckin' had it with the 3 circuit breakers under the seat and the 3 circuit breakers under the headlight nacelle, which could go out and kill the bike at any unsuspecting moment, even in Dallas rush hour traffic on the way to my carpenter apprentice school when everybody was mad as hell during the 1970s gas shortage, hahaha.

And as for that fuckin' little chrome box in front of the motor they called the Rectifier/Regulator Module,... I'd been through 3 of those suckers at this point in time, and they were 84 bucks each at the dealer when my house payment was 104. The electric starter never worked, unless you consider clouds of smoke coming up to be 'working' hahaha, and the disc brakes sucked ass, the rear rotor was warped from the factory, and the pawl on the kicker gear would bust off inside the kicker cover and make the kicker arm unwind on the spring cuz it no longer had the pawl to make it stop in the correct position. I went through 3 of those pawl things too. I guess 3 musta been the magic number for busted things on this bike.

Meanwhile,...the older guys in their late 20s and early 30s at the bike shops and bike bars were laughing at me, saying shit like "Told ya that you shoulda gotten an old Panhead chopper" or "I warned you not to buy that bowling ball bike shit." "You coulda got a nice Knuckle chopper at Brown's Custom Cycle for less than you paid for that piece of shit." And the old standard "AMF makes fuckin' bowling balls, they don't know shit about making dependable motorcycles."

But on the flip side, I had Stan talking to me. Now Stan was originally from Spartanburg South Carolina, but he had relocated to Dallas a few years before I met him through Shelby. Stan was a long haul trucker as well as being an experienced long haul chopper pilot, and had even been a roadie for Marshall Tucker Band so he'd been everywhere.

Stan's chopper was a beautiful work of art. And Shelby had just rebuilt it for him while Stan was in the Gray Bar Hotel, busted for a big weed possession. And I ain't got one damn photo of Stan's chopper. It was in an old Harley frame, raked and molded, looked mostly black to me, but it may have had some pearl sprayed in. Like I said before, got no photo of it, but the motor was a Pan lower with Shovelheads.

Stan is the one that told me "Don't listen to all those other guys. There is all kinds of untapped power in your motor. And those Shovelheads breathe better than the Pans, and those Shovels are the future. Your alternator is better than their generators. All you need to do is tear it all down and rebuild yourself a good handling dependable chopper. Get rid of all the shit that has ever caused a problem."

So I did.

Shelby helped out a lot. He knew an older mid 30s guy in Dallas that was wanting to get rid of his rigid frame and get a swing arm cuz he had back issues. And I was just the 20 year old guy wanting to get rid of my swing arm frame. So we did the swap. I gave the guy my AMF Shit frame and he gave me a nice used 1971 D&D Jammer frame, and now it was on. We also switched oil tanks cuz neither tank would fit on the new frames we swapped for. Then I went to a Scorpions swap meet in Dallas and picked up the other pieces for the chassis.

Meanwhile,… Shelby has my 74 AMF motor and tranny, tore it all the way down. He put in S&S stroker flywheels for me, the 4 & 1/2 inch ones. Shelby said if I went bigger with the 4 & 3/4 stroke, it might vibrate a lot and give me some issues out on the road and I knew I was gonna be doing lots of road trips on this new creation. So I took Guru Shelby's advice and stuck with the 4 & 1/2 stroke. S&S pistons, Andrews B grind cam, big 44 mm Mikuni carb and polished intake by Jerry Branch Flowmetrics, and the tranny was all done up with Andrews gears and equipped with a Barnett clutch.

Also at this time in 1975, Shelby was the first person I had seen with a belt drive on his 1939 Flathead 80 chopper. When he explained to me how it was less weight, less vibration, and easy to work with,…well I just HAD to have one. So I got one. Now I ain't saying this Phase 3 is only the second belt drive in Dallas back then, what I am saying is,…it is the second belt drive I ever knew about, so this is definitely some 'high tech action' back then, hahaha. So this is what it's looking like in late summer early fall, the tear down, 1975 in Dallas.

PART 43: "THE EARLY YEARS"

Fall of 1975

After I tore apart the swing arm version of the 74 AMF and got rid of the stock factory crapola, I hauled the old used 1971 D&D Jammer frame home in my 1968 Mustang. Then I flew in to work, building up my first chopper, which is now a stroker for better or worse, and this is what it started to look like. It's a "Swap Meet Special." Some might call it a rat chop, wink, wink. It's my first attempt, so gimme a break, OK?

As you can see, the motor and tranny came back from Shelby's shop, Mid Cities Choppers, and the rocker boxes even got some shiny stuff on 'em. Kool, hahaha. Where the clutch cable now runs, it got kinda too close for comfort touching the hot motor, so I brought home a chunk of electrical flex I found on the floor, painted it black, and slid it over the clutch cable for protection. Classy, eh? At this point, it still has an ignition switch on it, I hadn't done the toggle switch route just yet and it is still a hand clutch. And Phase 3, as far as I remember, had not come out with those protective shrouds that go around the alternator yet, so I'm just runnin' it bare at this stage.

To those with a sharp eagle eye, yes, that is an electric starter ring on the back Phase 3 pulley. Why? Cuz when Shelby asked me what the bike was, out of habit, I told him it was a 1974 FXE, so they sent me a belt drive set up for an electric start motor, hahaha. I kept it anyhow. Big deal. And those #1 foot pegs are the same ones I still run today. And those are the old stroker spacer plates sittin' under the cylinders. Who remembers them puppies?

And the $84 stock Harley chrome box Rectifier/Regulator Module has now been replaced with one of those ultra kool Sebring

Battery Eliminators. That's right, no more battery for me. The Sebring unit took the AC current from the alternator and converted it to run the bike's electrics. Only thing was, if the motor wasn't turning over, you ain't got no power. So you can't just turn on the lights like before if the motor is off. But the instant you kick it and the alternator first turns, it makes its own electrical power. And the front end is now a +15 inch over Twisted Springer with a 21 inch spool hub,...no front brake.

PART 44: "THE EARLY YEARS"

Fall of 1975

Whatever happened to the original 1974 AMF Super Glide Speedo & Tach? Why I've had it in a box all these years.

RIP, poor Speedo & Tach.
July 11, 1974 - September 1975

You rode out on the highways a grand total of 14 months and racked up 19,993 miles in that time. Too bad I didn't ride ya for another 7 miles to make it 20,000 even, huh? Not bad total miles for a 19-20 year old kid to cover across the US of A.

Part 45: "The Early Years"

Fall of 1975

Now some folks might think this is total bullshit, but it is what happened, hah. Out of the 74 AMF Shovel, I built this first chopper in about one month flat. That's right. From bare frame to Shelby stroking the motor and his buddy Harold doing the tranny and me doing the rest. Granted, it was a rattle can paint job, and the next few builds would also be rattle can builds, but it got me down the road and had a bit of class, or so the older guys told me, hahaha.

And that one month build also included getting some chrome work done. Even I have trouble believing this time line for the build today. Especially since the recent build on the 67 Shovel took me 1 year and 9 months through the covid shutdown.

And for more unasked for useless trivia, from 1974 until the build of 1989, the longest this Shovel was ever down was 5 weeks and 6 days, and that included 4 more bare frame up builds with a cut frame neck, to boot. No way could I do that today. So I don't blame you if you don't believe me, cuz I might not either, hah.

This photo here is the tail section of the 1971 D&D Jammer frame, which I still ride today, 48 years later. And that Bombay Taxi Horn came from Pier 1 Imports, think I paid $3.95 for it, if I remember right. And it kept me legal, cuz I no longer got an electric horn. Shelby told me if I didn't wanna get pulled over and ticketed, I'd better get something on it for a horn, so I did. And that is it. And it worked. So there ya go, copper.

At this stage I've got the seat and sissy bar set up pretty good and I'm doing a mechanical brake for the first time in my life, and I still run that today. The tail light wiring here is not exactly what the bike mags back then called 'super sano' but they did work. I duct taped them up to the bottom of the fender, which worked just fine,…until I'd get caught in the massive Texas rain storms and get them wet and they fell down on the tire. How many of ya have had that shit happen? That's why I run the wires inside a chrome tube today siliconed to the bottom side of the fender. See there? That's called 'live and learn.' And I did run a chain guard for a while, until I decided they were too much excess weight.

Part 46: "The Early Years"

Fall of 1975

For the front end I put on this used +15" over twisted springer with a 21 inch wheel with Avon Speedmaster rubber, no front brake, 6 inch risers with drag bars and the standard round Bates style chopper headlight. No more stock 74 AMF headlight for me with those 3 circuit breakers going off, shutting down the bike just to irritate me, wink, wink.

The gas tank was a Dallas swap meet special and that is the big honkin' 44 mm Mikuni carb from Jerry Branch Flowmetrics hangin' off the side to feed the new 84 inches of S&S Shovelhead motor. Now it's almost ready to ride out the front door of the house and go have some fun at the bars, swap meets and runs.

Part 47: "The Early Years"

Fall of 1975

On this special Friday after work I dropped off the paycheck at the bank, got some cash to make it through the weekend,… remember them pre-ATM days?…went by the booze store, grabbed a burger at the joint next to the likker store and came home all excited to get the 74 AMF Chopper running that very night. This would be its Maiden Voyage.

I finished up what little was left of the wiring. Then I went out to the garage and grabbed my lawn mower gas can (which was made outta real steel back then) and put some Ethyl in the chopper gas tank and then I filled up the original Harley chrome horseshoe oil tank with some nice fresh 50 weight, then I filled up the tranny. Since the motor and tranny were new builds, they were bone dry. OK, now it's time for the Test Run to see how the new chopper would ride.

I rolled it through the little living room, propped the front storm door open, set up my trusty plank and rolled the new creation down into the front yard. This was getting very exciting. I felt like a little kid on Christmas. I realize I had already been on two long cross country trips, the one to Canada on the 67 Sportster in 1973 and then the recent one from 3 or 4 months ago on the 1974 Super Glide, but those were on stock bikes the factory made. This experience here was gonna be totally different.

After I kicked over the new motor a few times, I turned on the key, kicked a bit more and then that sucker fired right up! Yay! "It's Alive!" How sweet it sounded to me. I was babyin' the throttle a bit, then I let it sit and idle for a minute or so, checking to see how it idled and looking to see if there were any leaks in the fuel line or in the 3 oil lines. So far it was bone dry. Good.

So next I plopped my butt down in the new/used 20 dollar swap meet seat, pulled in the clutch, stuck it in gear and off I rode on the new chopper. I rode a looong ways, all around the entire fuckin' block…

Then I rolled up into the front yard, got off and watched it idle some more and checked for any leaks. Still bone dry. Good again. By this time the sun had gone down and there were some little kids, a few teenagers, and a coupla little old annoyed neighbor ladies next door lookin' out to see what all the new racket was.

They were used to the Super Glide living here the past year, and I suppose they even got used to seeing it rolling in and out of the house, but the Super Glide was a fairly civilized bike with semi-quiet pipes. This stroker chopper beast here was blasting out exhaust through some old used straight drag pipes, the extra short kind, cuz the rigid frame needed some pipes to fit the rigid frame, so Shelby helped me out with a good deal on the used short open drags. I was standing there wonderin' just how many cops would also like these new shorty drags.

Things were still looking good on the chopper. No leaks anywhere and the wiring seemed to be doing OK. The lights stayed on, the Sebring Battery Eliminator gizmo must be doin' its thing, so off we go again. This time I headed for Main Street Highway 80 and rode maybe a mile or so to the east headed toward Dallas, then circled around and came back home and checked it again. Still good to go. I decided that was enough test ride for the first night, kinda felt a little bit uneasy riding a brand new motor and a brand new tranny on a brand new chopper build in the dark of night, ya know? So I didn't wanna do anymore ridin' on the new build and new motor until it was sunny again, and the next day was Saturday and there'd be plenty of time for riding tomorrow.

So now it's time to fuckin' celebrate, even if I was all by myself, hahaha. I didn't want anybody else around this night in case the 74 AMF Chopper turned out to be a Big Fail and maybe not even start and run, if ya know what I mean? Or what if it fired to life and then burst into flames? I didn't want anybody around me this special night, no gal friend, no brother, no cuzzins, no riding friends, just the new chopper and me. This was just our First Date Night.

Next I rolled the new chopper back up the plank to go back inside the house and I parked it back in its own room. This was a little tiny crackerbox house, just two little bedrooms, one for it and one for me, that's all. Now if you were around in 1975 and remember what that year was like,...this is what it was also like for me. I was 20 with my own house, just built my first chopper which had just fired to life for the first time, had just gotten the brand new 1975 Technics Stereo setup, turntable, amp, and their SB 5000-A Speakers. There was a brand new band out called Bad Company and their first album was blastin' outta them Technics speakers, plus I had some Columbian Gold and the coldest beer in town sat in the fridge just waitin' for me.

So I moseyed over to my ever expanding record collection which was in 4 piles leaning up against each other in alphabetical order on the floor and I dug out Led Zepplin's newest album, Physical Graffiti. You can probably guess what I'm up to now. Opened up the double album cover and dumped out the Columbian Gold on it to separate the stems and seeds,...just like you used to do,...right, hahaha? And hey, this was high dollar weed back then, cuz I shelled out 30 whole bucks for that lid. And that's how the first night with the new 74 AMF Chopper went for me. I sat there on the couch smokin' weed, drinkin' beer, listening to tunes blasting and I stared at the new chopper creation right in front of me for a looong time into the night.

The next morning, I woke up and rode the new chopper over to Emma's Truck Stop on Highway 80 in Grand Prairie and had me a Celebration Breakfast which was Chicken Fried Steak with Cream Gravy and 3 Eggs and Hash Browns, yum, yum. When it got to be around 10 o'clock I rode over to Shelby's shop, Mid Cities Choppers and parked the new thing I built outside his front shop door.

Maybe I was kinda overzealous, or expecting too much, cuz I thought a coupla guys would come out and check what I'd been building the last 4 weeks. But they didn't really seem to give a rat's ass, hahaha. Maybe they got their own problems? And then? And then Shelby came out and looked at it and said I did good.

And before he walked back into his shop to his customers, he said "C'mon by the shop at closing time today and we'll go get a beer or two." I got blown away with that one. Next I kicked the chopper to life and rode it over to downtown Dallas to Brown's Custom Cycles and saw Jesse and his two boys. Conley's H-D dealer was still next door to Brown's back then, and Catalina Cycle and Pool's were also on that same intersection on East Main Street. So I kinda hung out with the other guys on choppers for a bit. Now I felt like I was kinda fittin' in with the 'Build What You Ride, Ride What You Build' crowd. I had finally done it, and there it sat for proof.

Next I rode it over to Ivey's H-D dealer where I bought the 74 brand new, when they were still in Grand Prairie, where Joe Cox was working as head mechanic. I rode right up, parked the chopper and walked back to the shop and asked Joe to come out and look at what I had just done.

Joe was wiping his hands with a red shop rag as he walked out with me, then Joe groaned really loud and started laughing. Then he shook his head and sez, "Ya know, Dave, back in 1958 when Harley finally came out with a swing arm frame, the entire Harley world rejoiced. Now you just set progress back 20 years in time." So that's how much Joe liked my new Rigid Framed Creation, hahaha.

When it got to be shop closing time that afternoon, I rode back over to Shelby's shop. When Shelby had said we'll go for a beer or two, I had no idea where he meant. Around the corner? Down to the County Line where the bars were? Nope. He said we're ridin' over to a bar in Fort Worth. Hmm,… OK, that sounds good to me.

We rode west on Highway 80 passed where Ivey's was on the other side of the rail road tracks, passed The Shadows Tavern which was one of my old hangouts, then on through Arlington, and back then the towns weren't all solid concrete with strip malls like today. Ridin' along with Shelby on his 80 inch Flathead Chopper was amazing. I could not have been any more blown away if I was riding with Peter Fonda and Dennis Hopper or riding with Ron Finch and Arlen Ness. Shelby had his own riding style like nobody else I've seen since. First off, I don't remember ever seeing Shelby in jeans. He wore green or tan Khakis, a t shirt from his own chopper shop, and,…get ready for it,…sandals. That's right, Shelby wore Jesus Boots. He kicked his chopper wearin' his old leather sandals. His Flathead Chopper looked kinda like a Super Glide from 50 yards, cuz he ran a narrow glide on it. But the closer you got to it, the more trick work you saw on it. When Shelby was riding he kept his right hand on the throttle of course, but he always kept his left hand on his right shoulder… unless he was shiftin' his jockey shift.

Shelby had a pony tail nearly down to his belt which blew out behind him, and he shaved his chin but had really long sideburns and a big handlebar mustache, and he always looked at me over the tops of his aviator glasses. I rode to the right side of Shelby in our lane and I made sure to keep my front wheel maybe 3 or 4 feet behind Shelby's front wheel, out of respect. Shelby was the Chopper Star, the Flathead Guru, I was simply the back up guy tryin' to learn the chopper ropes from him and his pals.

After we putted through the downtown part of Arlington, we actually rode along for a while with woods on both sides of the highway until we got into the edge of Fort Worth. And? There it was. The first real biker bar I had ever seen. And the word "biker" has been sooo over-used these days that I don't even use the word anymore. I simply refer to myself as a 'chopper builder.' That about sums it up.

So Shelby and me are downshifting, pulling into this bar that I no longer remember the name of. If any of you folks reading this remember Fort Worth Chopper Lore, this bar was on the far east side of Fort Worth, was a dark gray rectangular building and sat on the south side of the road, had a big gravel parking lot, and on this Saturday night musta had 30 or so choppers parked in the lot, with maybe only 4 or 5 cars. When we pulled into the lot with our tires crunching in the gravel, Shelby stuck his Flattie in neutral and started backing up his chop so I fell in line next to him, backing mine up next to his. When the other folks standing outside saw Shelby pulling in, a little crowd of guys and their ol' ladies came walking over and gathered around him, sayin' hi and shit like that. Now I ain't claimin' it was like being with Elvis, but it was sorta close to it.

Now here is where I felt kinda funny and miserably outta place. All these guys and gals were probably in their 30s or so and they were

THE EARLY YEARS

riding old tried and true authentic road-worn choppers, like Flatties, Knuckles, Pans, Triumphs, Indians, chopper fodder such as that.

And here I am, the young 20-year-old punk kid on the chopper with the still new-ish AMF Cone Motor. See where I'm going with this? Although I am now riding a scratch-built chopper I did myself, it still carries the cursed AMF Bowling Ball Stigma, that shiny fuckin' cone on the bottom of the motor stuck out like a sore fuckin' thumb in the parking lot lights and moonlight. Rat farts. Donkey shit. See what happened there? If my motor had been an old 1966 to 1969 Genny Shovel or Pan bottom, then I mighta fit right in. But,…it wasn't, and I didn't, hardy har har.

But just then as I'm feelin' kinda nervous about stickin' out so much, Shelby broke the ice for me and told one of the guys how he just built that hot rod stroker motor for me. So that gave me a little tiny bit of class, shall we say? And then when the other guys that were milling around started looking at my new creation, I think it mighta fooled them a little bit cuz it didn't look "new" at all, cuz it was built outta old parts, get what I mean? Although it was only a day old, the used swap meet parts made it look like it had been around some already. And then they saw the Phase 3 open belt drive set up and got a bit more interested. All in all it turned out to be a good night for the 74 AMF Chopper's Maiden Voyage. And the fact that I could shoot pool purdy good and had them Columbian Gold joints with me didn't hurt my chances with the new guys none, either.

When we were getting ready to ride out a few hours later at bar time, I was proud to be walking up to my home made 74 AMF Chopper, even though it was a rattle can bowling ball build, I liked it and it rode pretty good. And sitting there backed in next to Shelby's Flattie, the moonlight was shining down on the front twisted legs on the +15 over springer. I wish to hell I had some pictures from that night. But,… Shelby had strict orders of 'no fuckin' cameras' any time we rode anywhere. And I did what I was told. So this photo here is my 'First Chopper Build' and yes, that is my old sleepin' bag in the corner, ready to go road trippin' again.

SHOVELHEAD DAVE

Part 48: "The Early Years"

Bicentennial 1976

The in-their-30s 'older' group of Dallas chopper folks sorta took me in,…kinda like an illegitimate step child,… I suppose, hah.

I got to go ridin' with them to the fun chopper bars in Dallas and Fort Worth, and the area swap meets, which were a blast.

According to legend, Shelby had 8 Flathead 80s at the time. He had his main ride black rigid chopper, plus a really fancy chrome and gold plated long show chopper he used to show in Dallas at the World of Wheels, then 2 more 80 inch Flatties in stock condition, and he had the frames and motors and trannys for the other 4, disassembled in his shop, scattered around a little bit.

Meanwhile, Harold, one of Shelby's best buddies rode a really nice chopped Panhead, one of the nicest in the area if ya ask me. It had lots of chrome and a nice loooong Durfee girder on it. Harold was a machinist by trade and worked for Bell Helicopter over in Arlington.

Stan was originally from Spartanburg South Carolina, was a long haul truck driver who had relocated to Dallas, but he was in the Gray Bar Hotel waiting to get out for some illegal devil weed stuff. Stan rode a fine chopped Panhead lower end with Shovel heads, and it was stashed at Shelby's shop. And it is Stan's fault that I have kept the 74 AMF Chopper all these years, he told me to believe in those Shovelheads.

Blue was half Irish and half Cherokee, rode a red Knuckle 1941 FL. He had just redone it up fresh, motor and tranny, and also had an original side car with it. Blue was also a machinist in Irving and he is the guy that used to make those Bronze Cast Wing Plaques that used to sell in the ads in the back of Easyriders magazine. I have mine out on the garage wall right now,…where's yours, wink, wink?

Slick was a big bald headed guy (Slick, get it?) with a big bushy red beard, rode a swing arm Panhead chop with custom paint work done on it and his ol' ladies' name was Possum.

And now that is the little group I kinda luckily fell in with riding in Dallas in 1976. This photo here is Shelby sitting down, wearing his famous shop T Shirt (and I still have mine). and his wife Gloria, is on the far left side in the black t shirt, that's Gloria's hippie gal pal Gail in the center with Harold's wife Janet. These ultra-kool folks also helped to make up the first of the Dallas ABATE group, and Blue was President.

Part 49: "The Early Years"

Bicentennial 1976

Goin' on into the spring of 1976 I hadn't done any long road trips in 8 or 9 moths now. Well,...by 'long' road trips I mean road trips that went several states away, like 2,000 to 4,000 mile trips. I rode the +15" over Twisted Springer 74 AMF Chopper around Texas, down to the Gulf, Padre Island and Galveston. Or I'd ride it over to visit Cuzzin Johnny and other relatives in Oklahoma and Texarkana, up into the Ozarks through Hot Springs and Fayetteville Arkansas. And once I rode it into the southern bottom of Missouri, to their purdy Bull Shoals Lake area, smaller weekend-type trips like that, or 3 day trips if it was a holiday weekend or I got laid off for a coupla days or three.

And I'd ride with Brudder Charles on his 71 Shovelhead and my buddy Freddie who was on my old Red 67 Sportster I had sold him in the spring of 1974, and Gary on his Black 1975 Sportster. and Ray and Debra around the corner on their Black 1972 Super Glide. So, I still had my old riding buddies as well as my new chopper ridin' buddies. So I was gettin' out on the new chopper, just not ridin' really far away yet.

And, noooooo,...don't you even dare to think of it, bwahaha! It's not that I was a-skeered to ride somethin' far away that I had built my own damn self, hahaha, I was actually kinda busy working on construction jobs in Dallas. So my campin' road trip rides were limited to the general Texas area, but there was one thing that these trips showed me.

Ummmmmm,... I didn't really like that Twisted Springer.

There, I said it, it looked fine, I LOVED the way it looked. But it was very bouncy, if ya know what I mean? Maybe I shoulda looked into seeing if I coulda gotten it to stiffen up a bit, but I never did. Going in a straight line was fine, it rode great. But going into a little bump, like the curb/gutter thing ya ride into when ya pull in for gas? Just little shit like that, or potholes in the roads? And a pothole or bigger bump while leanin' into the corner doing 50 or so could get downright scary, hahaha. The springer would hit the bump and then 'bounce, bounce, bounce' until it settled down on its own. I tried tightenin' up the bolts on the rockers, but it did not help. And this springer did not have a shock on it, just rode on the springs. Hmm. What to do? And then?

And then came the spring swap, the ABATE Swap Meet over in Dallas and I went to it and there I found 'The Answer to my Bouncing Problems'. Yep, there it was, leaning up on this guy's table. A +25" over Flame Cut Girder! How fuckin' kool is that shit?

It was only a hunnerd bucks. So I got it. I'd been workin' fairly steady and was sorta flush with some cash-o-la. This was my 3rd year into the carpenter apprentice trade so I was making almost what a real journeyman carpenter made…yay! (Almost…but not quite, hah.) The hunnerd bucks was no biggie for me then. So now I'm luggin' around this heavy ass +25" over Flame Cut Plate Steel Girder slung over my shoulder diggin' a hole in me, and I'm 6 foot 4 and that damn thing is about as long as I am tall, hahaha.

But wait! There's more! What's that shiny thing over yonder? Oh my gawd, wouldya look at that purdy thang? Why,…that's one of them fuckin' Invader 5 Spoke mag wheels that I done- seen in them chopper magazines. Gotta have that, right? It was only 50 bucks, what a fuckin' good deal, plus it had a nice and nearly brand new Avon Speedmaster tire on it, to boot.

So now I'm gonna go back home and put all this new found swap meet treasure on the 74 AMF Chopper,…just as soon as I get back from celebratin' these new finds at the local waterin' hole.

In this photo I had just yanked off the +15" over Twisted Springer,…sniff, sniff,…and gettin' ready to put that new looong girder on it. And check out my new home made welded pipe lift. Purdy classy, eh? I copied the lift Shelby loaned me and made one like it and it's still out in the garage today.

THE EARLY YEARS

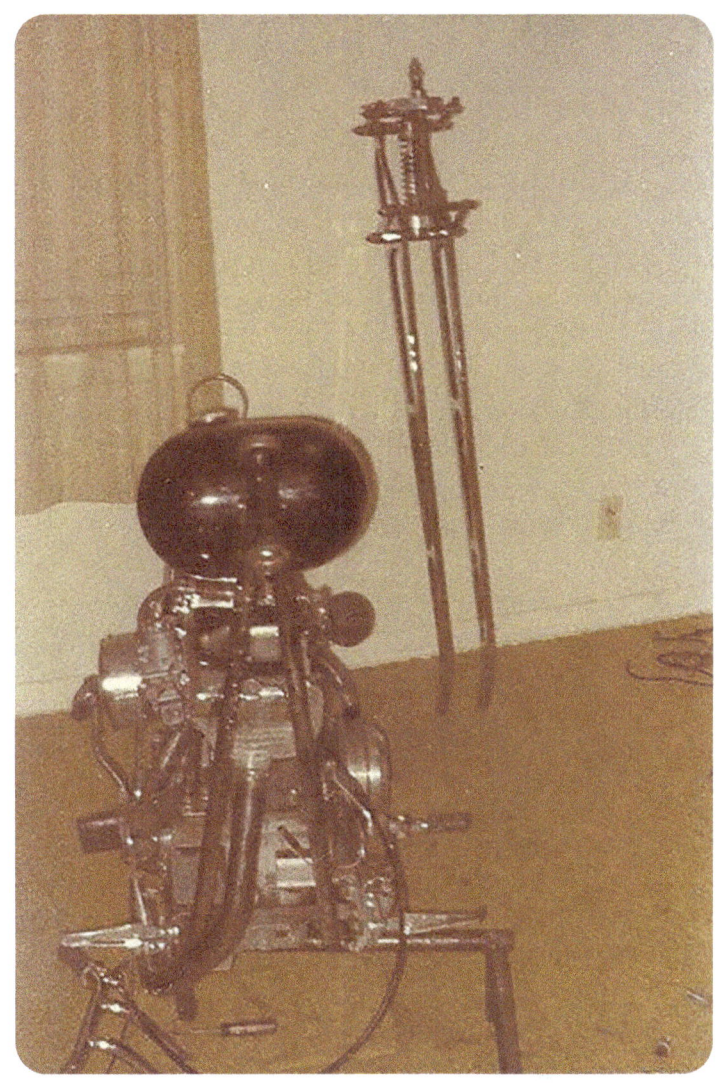

PART 50: "THE EARLY YEARS"

Sometime in Bicentennial 1976

Dear Folks, here's Harold on his Panhead Chopper,… RIP. He was one of the funniest and smartest chopper guys I ever knew, and he had that dry-wry witty sense of humor that I admired soooo fuckin' much. He could be just fuckin' gruesome at times, hahaha. I've seen Harold snidely cut down and shame some non motorsickle ridin' dorks sooo fuckin' bad that the dorks didn't even know it happened. We'd start bustin' a gut laughin' and the dorks would be like,… "Huh? What's so funny?"

THE EARLY YEARS

Anyhow, one night,... Harold and Shelby took me on a 'Surprise Chopper Ride' over to this umm,..."club",...shall we call it, over in Arlington, Texas, just outside Fort Worth on Highway 80,...they mighta called it Division Street over there? Now this wasn't no ordinary drinkin' club to shoot pool and play the juke box, and it was not for the lightweights and wusses, and it wasn't no regular topless titty club. This was a Gentlemen's Club and after we backed our three choppers into their curb, they let us in even though we weren't exactly gentlemen. The big bouncer guy at the door acted like he actually knew Shelby and Harold really good, like maybe they had been there before? Maybe?

So Harold and Shelby showed their membership cards and I had to get one, and yes I was 21 at this time, had just turned 21 as a matter of fact, so now I was of legal tender age. Regular bars you could get in when you were 18 back then, and I was always big enough and looked old enough that I was getting into some of the bars when I was 16, hahaha. Plus I could drive through those Drive Thru Beer Barns they had all over Dallas and get cases of beer when I was 16 and 17, so I was used to drinkin' a little bit by then.

Texas has (or at least had) some really strange laws when it comes to drinking and titties,... I mean,...lady boobs. And this place that Harold and Shelby took me to was not just a topless joint. This joint was a "fully nekked bar." That's right. Those poor gals' clothes would fall off right in front of you, and I'm talking about a classy strip joint where the high class gals went down all the way. And they'd show you their poo-nanner in an old timey seductive burlesque strip-tease manner, not like these talentless pole dancing floozies and skeezers they got today what-with the fake boobs an' all. This was a real stripper club with real classy strippers with real strippin' boobs.

But here's the deal. In Texas back then, if the strippers were gonna go all the way down to totally butt nekked,...and these did,... then the afore mentioned strip joint could NOT sell any booze. That's right. We had to bring our own bottles of booze.

And if you were a beer drinker, you had to bring your own beer into the joint. But who wants to carry all that heavy beer when a bottle of hooch will do just fine and weigh less on the chopper,... right? Right.

So we went in and got a table right up front close to the stage action. Now for the Rip Off Part. OK so we are sitting there with our bottles of booze, and this purdy gal with big hooters comes up, bends over to the point that her two things nearly fell out, and she asks Shelby and Harold and me what we want for mixers. We were keepin' it simple and ordering Cokes cuz we brought our good buddy Jack Daniel's with us,…cuz we were kinda classy our own damn selves, hahaha.

Then the purdy gal comes back and sets three glasses of ice down in front of us with three bottles of Cokes,…yes, they still had bottles back then,…and then she tells us the outrageous

price, hahaha. I forget what it was, but like 12 or 15 bucks or so for the 3 of us. I was flabbergasted. It'd be much, much cheaper to buy mixed drinks at a regular bar, but the entertainment wouldn't be as classy, eh? Lemme think about that one,…umm,…titties vs juke box? Poo-nanner vs pool table?

I will never forget the dancing gal named Sandy who came out on stage, hahaha. Here it is, 46 years later and I'm still talkin' about her. She was what they used to call a "Buxom Blonde" a real one, lemme tell ya, cuz I was a witness to the entire down under show. She had real blonde hair down to the middle of her back and those big blue peepers and full red lips with nice big purdy jiggly jugs.

She was slowly writhin' and undulatin' like a slinky horny snake,… I guess you could call it dancin',…to Nazareth's "Love

Hurts" and the way she did it, I'm sure it did hurt, hahaha. Her mammaries were huge enough that she could bend forward and gather them up like a Mama Hen gathers up her little chicks, then Sandy would take a cowboy hat off any cowboy who was lucky enough to be sittin' up front like us, (there's always cowboys in Texas bars) and she'd wiggle her boobs and put 'em inside the hat. And then? And then she'd stand up and walk around with the hat sticking on like magic. Now THAT is talent. So that is how I got introduced to Shelby's and Harold's favorite hang out, bwahahaha. And don't tell my folks cuz they'd get all mad an' shit and say I was hangin' out with hoodlums and hussies.

Part 51: "The Early Years"

Sometime in Bicentennial 1976

Here's another picture switchin' the +15" over Twisted Springer out and putting the +25" over Flame Cut Girder on. And now I got the good bike stand, slide it under the chopper, then flip it and you can raise either the front end or back end of the bike. Ya just can't do both at the same time.

PART 52: "THE EARLY YEARS"

Bicentennial 1976

Before I forget, since 1976 was the year I turned 21, I got myself a 21st birthday present I had wanted since I was a little kid,…a 1963 Sting Ray. Ain't it a beauty? This is what 1800 bucks got you back in 1976. It's got a 327 engine, 4 speed, convertible with both tops although the rag top was literally rags, a Wonderbar AM radio that actually worked, and it had power steering and power brakes. A cop in Irving Texas had been drag racing it, cuz it had the 340 hp solid lifter set up in it.

THE EARLY YEARS

Now let's investigate this a little bit and see what your hard earned bucks got you back then. My folks were against everything I ever did, chopper and car wise, so they never gave me one nickel in my shenanigans. And I wasn't even a full-fledged carpenter yet, just an apprentice making about 6 bucks an hour.

And on those 6 bucks an hour I got my own house, the 74 AMF Chopper, a Red 1968 Mustang and now this Rat '63 Sting Ray. It would be impossible to do any of that today. But back then, with just one week's paycheck, I could pay the house payment and all the utilities, and then I still had 3 more paychecks that month to do what I wanted, and today? It takes 2 carpenter paychecks to make one house payment and another paycheck to pay the utilities…groan. I wanna go back to the 1970s, hahaha.

Part 53: "The Early Years"

Bicentennial 1976

So here's what the 74 AMF Chopper wound up looking like for Bicentennial 1976. This is the version I was riding with the Dallas guys out to runs, ABATE stuff, swap meets and local bars having fun. They introduced me to Mother Blues kick ass bar in Dallas and then sometimes we'd ride over to the Mother Lode bar in Fort Worth to watch live bands.

This was also about the time that Easyriders magazine was working with the MCs in different cities around the country putting on swap meets. Those were some fun times as well. In Dallas it was Easyriders/Scorpions Swap Meets. Many of the parts on the 74 AMF Chopper even still today came from those 1970s swaps, hahaha.

Here we have the +25" over swap meet girder and the swap meet 5 Spoke Invader front wheel, no brake, just spinnin' out front. The girder was so slim that for wheel spacers, I just used a washer on each side. Ain't got the head light on just yet, but it was a round one that I ran. I realize the front end of the frame is kicked up a bit too much, but what the hell? It was a loooong ass bike and that's what I wanted at that time. From the back of the back tire to the front of the front tire it was 11 feet and 7 inches long. That was always easy for me to remember cuz it's the opposite of the 7-11 stores.

And this is the version that is gonna ride to Daytona 1977 in just a few months from this photo.

THE EARLY YEARS

PART 54: "THE EARLY YEARS"

End of Bicentennial 1976

The Bicentennial Year of 1976 ended with my chance to meet a guy from Portland Oregon named Tom (M) who was an older Brother Speed MC member. Tom had the bucks, moved into town with a fine young lady, opened a business selling other businesses their paper products, got a nice house in Arlington and had Shelby build him up a Custom Panhead.

Tom's Panhead was totally scratch built by Shelby. I do not have one single photo of it, dammit. So I'll try going from memory. Seems to me the swing arm frame was kind of a dark chocolate brown while the gas tank and fenders were painted in a gold- ish bronze color. The front end was a wide glide maybe 6 or 8 inches over. It was a beautiful work of art, had kick and electric start on it. This was the bike which Shelby was gonna ride to Daytona in a coupla months and show at the Rat's Hole Show. Tom wanted Shelby to ride it there and show it, so this was gonna be a big deal.

Just to give ya a head's up, this bike was soooo fuckin' fine that out of all the hunnerds of bikes entered in the show, this one took 4th Place at the Rat's Hole Show and won Most Unusual. Shelby had been working on this Panhead for a while and nearly had it finished by the end of 1976, just a few odds and ends for details.

Shelby had moved the Panhead over to Tom's and Sandy's(?) I think her name was? And on this night Shelby invited me to go along on his trip over there. When we got to their place, there was the Custom Panhead, sitting in the middle of their nice living room with the plush carpet. It was sitting there with overhead lights glowing on it like it was an altar,…cuz it was.

Tom had the finest green bud in town, and he lit up a big fattie. They had some drinks going, music playing and Sandy was our fine hostess. After we'd been there for a while just sittin' around, I asked Tom if I could check out the bike and he said sure. So I carefully dragged my stoned ass over next to the work of art and I sat there on the floor cross legged, checking out every detail on that bike that I could. I was amazed at Shelby's craftsmanship. I'd seen plenty of his bikes before, but this was something in a totally different class.

I slowly slid along the floor every few minutes to scoot down and take in another section of the Pan, then I moved around to the other side and did the same thing. Meanwhile, Shelby and Tom are sitting on the couch passin' the killer joint back and forth kinda laughing at me. Tom said somethin' like "Is that the first nice bike that kid's ever seen?" Shelby laughed. Then I said "It's certainly the finest bike I've ever seen."

And of course I never touched it. When I was done admiring their creation, I said "It's like if you took a pencil with an eraser on the end, and tried to touch any little spot on this bike, the spot you'd touch would be customized. There isn't even one tiny spot on this bike that hasn't been hand crafted."

Shelby and Tom kinda laughed and then Shelby said "Now you get it." I never forgot that night. Flash forward to 1992 in Seattle. I had a carpenter job doing the woodwork on a remodeled cruise ship called "The Spirit of Alaska" and it was a medium size ship that went up and down the Pacific Northwest, from Seattle to Anchorage. There was an older crew member on that ship I got to know. His arms were covered in battered worn out tats of the Harley Davidson variety. I asked him if he had ridden with a bike club. He said "Yeah,… I rode with one down in Portland, but you wouldn't have heard about it."

I asked him "Was it Brother Speed?" His eyes got big and he started laughing and he pointed at me and asked "Now how in the hell would a young guy like YOU know about Brother Speed?" I told him I knew his club brother Tom from when he moved down to Dallas in 1976 and had that gold colored Custom Panhead built by Shelby, and then we were good buddies from then on until that ship sailed away. Here's a photo of Harold's motor from 1976. Harold liked Schlitz Beer. Can ya tell?

SHOVELHEAD DAVE

PART 55: "THE EARLY YEARS"

February & March 1977

Just turned 22 now and was over at my second home, aka Mid Cities Choppers hangin' out with Shelby, Harold and the other guys. It was gettin' close to closin' time for Shelby and the folks started wandering away. Shelby was in the back part of the shop where his main work bench was and as I was also gettin' ready to split, when Shelby looked over at me and outta the blue sez "Ya know next month we are ridin' to Daytona for Bike Week. We don't normally let anyone as young as you ride with us,…but since you've been showin' some class, we decided to let you ride along if you wanna."

HOLY SHIT! REALLY? How unexpected. I couldn't believe what I just heard. I stood there kinda stunned and shocked for a coupla seconds, just takin' it in, and then told him of course,… I'd be honored to go. He kinda looked at me over the top of his glasses like he mighta been thinkin' to himself,…'now don't get all gooshy on me, it's only a Daytona bike trip'

I had a really extra happy ride on the way back home that evening, knowing I was gonna get to ride along with the real guys on a cross country road trip, going a few states away on the chopper I built myself. I had to let that sink in. And it sank in to the bottom just fine, hell yeah, I was ridin' to Daytona now… Fuckin' A.

When I got back to my little house, I was so goofy I started looking around trying to figure out what to pack, gathering up the tent and sleeping bag, and then it hit me…'hey dumb ass, you don't leave for several more days.' I'd been on plenty of cross country trips by this time, but those trips were with guys basically my own age on stock bikes. This was gonna be some totally different action.

Then I started to kinda panic. What if my rattle can 74 AMF Bowling Ball Chopper breaks down in front of these guys? How embarrassing would that be? What if the boss don't let me take off work? Well, fuck him then, I can always get another job, right? I started thinkin' how much money will I need to stash. And speaking of stash, I now had a nice place down inside the oil tank for my stash, cuz with the Sebring Battery Eliminator, the oil tank was empty without a battery in it. So that part was good to go.

I even pulled out my old Road Atlas map to look at, to see the roads we'd be taking on the choppers. I was kinda like a little kid looking at a Sears catalogue at the toys he wanted for Christmas,… but probably had a slim chance of gettin'.

Figuring out the distance, it looked like it was gonna be a little bit over 1,000 miles. I wondered if we'd make it in 2 days or 3? And how many guys would be going? And what all to pack clothes-wise, cuz there weren't no mountains involved this time. But,…it sometimes rains a lot that time of year there in the Gulf area.

In the next few days hangin' out at the shop, I found out the group would be Shelby on that new fancy Custom Panhead he just built for Tom, and Harold would be going on his awesome Panhead Chopper, then Stan was going on his Pan/Shovel Chop cuz he was now free from the Gray Bar Hotel, and both Harold's and Stan's kool choppers ran Durfee girders. And Blue was going on his nice Red Knuckle he'd just done with the side car. And Slick was in on the group, too. But Slick wasn't riding the trip, he was going in his Good Times Van, fancy painted up with the panels and pinstripes, you know, like the fun vans were in 1977. And Slick would take his swing arm Custom Pan inside his van. So now we had a haulin' device in case of any unfortunate breakdowns,…gulp. Would that be me?

The Departure Day came and I don't even remember the official day we left, too many years ago and I ain't got no pictures of it. Once again, Shelby insisted on NO FUCKIN' CAMERAS and I was not gonna violate his orders. So we ain't got no pictures. But I do remember it was kinda drizzly weather. And I also remember I had to pack the bike different this time than from all the other road trips before. First of all, it WAS a different bike, so it's gotta be packed a different way, I had to roll the tent up inside the sleeping bag like a burrito, then put both of them in the duffelbag on back, where there wasn't that much room.

And speakin' of putting them 'on back' I was now wishing I had gotten a higher sissy bar when I first put the 74 AMF into the rigid frame. Too late now, gotta make do. It was a tight fit, but I got everything on there. Then I looped another smaller bag up around the head light and it hung down on the +25" over girder. The tool bag I ran down low on the down tubes in front of the motor. Now for what to wear on this road trip? I had on my Greezy Jeans, you know the ones, the kind that repel water cuz ya ain't washed 'em in over a year, and I had on the black leather jacket and gloves. And now,… here's where the situation gets kinda goofy,…or actually a lot goofy.

I knew some of the older guys that rode and hung around at Shelby's shop had leather chaps. Well I ain't got none. And some of the older guys had those cool leather britches, like leather Levis. I ain't got none of them neither. So what DO I got? Oh nooooo. Groan. My old rodeo cowboy chaps! Yep, that's right. I drug out my old bull riding chaps from 1971 and was wearin' them things. You might think,…so what? Chaps are chaps,…right?

Wrong. Picture this in your mind. You got this old photo here to see what the 74 AMF Chop looked like. Now picture me on it wearing those rodeo chaps, and those cowboy chaps were Bright Royal Blue suede leather, fuzzy side out, and they were trimmed in maybe 4 inch long WHITE FRINGE with 3 big white stars going down the sides like the Dallas Cowboys Star, and then my big white leather initials "D A P" on the bottoms, bwahaha! Dang it, I'd give a hunnerd bucks for a picture of that goofy get up to laugh at right now.

A few years earlier in the Kowbell Rodeo Arena over in Mansfield, these chaps mighta been really cool lookin' while riding the bulls, with spurs a-flyin' an' shit like that. But here with these guys riding choppers to Daytona, instead of cool cowboy chaps they were more like my Rodeo Clown Chaps sittin' on the chopper. When we got ready to pull out, guess what happened? Guess who was the foolish clown from the git- go? I'm gonna give ya a clue.

Wide floppy cowboy chaps + open belt drive spinning = what?

If you guessed my chaps got caught in the open belt drive, you are the winner, we were all sittin' there idlin' away, ready to pull out on the most important run of my 22 year old life, and my rodeo chaps got caught up in the belt drive and kilt my motor right then and there in front of everybody, but wait, it gets worse. Not only is the 74 AMF engine now dead, my leg is also trapped inside the belt drive. So how awkward was it to try to put the kick stand down and get them chaps outta there? This ain't no easy thing to do. I'm trying to balance the 11 foot long- ass chopper, which is fully packed, and I only got one leg to use while I try to free myself from this dreadful humiliation. And Blue was right behind me on his Knuckle just laughing his ass off, bwahaha.

Shelby and Harold were up front and they musta been rollin' their eyes thinkin' to themselves 'what the hell kinda clown boy did we just invite along?' I eventually got the chaps free and pulled the left chap leg up higher so it would be further away from the belt drive. Got the 74 AMF kicked over again and,…we're off!

Shelby and Harold were ridin' up front, Stan and me next in line, and then Blue was behind us cuz his Knuckle and side car took up a whole lane like a car, so he was good to go in his own lane.

And then Slick brought up the rear in his Good Times Van. And like I said earlier, I ain't got any action photos of this actual trip, but I do have photos from that same time frame just before and after the trip and I have some pictures of the souvenirs I got from Daytona, so we're gonna hafta make do with them for this road trip chapter. And don't blame me for not having any gawddamn pictures cuz I wanted to take the damn camera, hahaha! This picture is in my front yard and there is my ridin' buddy Mike's 1976 White Super Glide.

THE EARLY YEARS

PART 56: "THE EARLY YEARS"

A Wet Ride to Daytona 1977

Before I go any further in this semi-boring riding to Daytona segment, I gotta stop for one of those old timey station identification things they used to do on TV. This is not a commercial though. It is a confession.

While Harold, Stan, and Slick have left us now,…(RIP) the last I heard, good ol' Shelby and Blue are still with us and doing OK. And there might be the slightest snowball-in-hell tiny chance that they may read this account of our trip someday. And if they do, I want them and everybody else reading this drivel to know that I have tried my utmost best to stay pin-point accurate in all the slimey details on this sordid and kinda disastrous Daytona adventure.

That also means in order to tell the 100% truth, it is gonna make me look bad a coupla times. Yes,…that's right, I am gonna rat myself out for you. I am gonna take you down to the depths of my despair and humiliation. But before you think I was a total wuss that wimped out, all I ask is that you try to remember that I had just turned 22 years old, was riding only the 2nd chopper I built so far, and was on my first cross country chopper road trip with the for-real chopper guys who were building and riding choppers back in the 1960s. In other words, let's try to remember I was a newbie tryin' to hang with the real guys, OK? Awright, now that this confession time is over, let's get back to our regularly scheduled program,… A Wet Ride to Daytona.

So our group of 5 bikes and the Good Times Van started up the rainy wet road leaving Dallas,…right after I got the cowboy chaps untangled from the open belt drive, hahaha. The formation we rode in was Shelby leading the pack on the beautiful Custom Panhead he had built for Tom, and Shelby was in the left side of the lane with Harold on his Durfee Panhead chopper to Shelby's right, then Stan on his Durfee Pan/Shovel was following Shelby and I was behind Harold on my AMF Bowling Ball Bike with the +25" over girder. Then Blue was following us on his beautiful Red Knuckle with the side car. Inside Blue's side car was his regular camping gear plus a whole bunch of his Harley Wings Plaques he sold at swap meets and advertised in the back of Easyriders magazine, back in those old tan colored pages. Behind Blue was Slick in his custom painted van with his swing arm Panhead inside. It's raining so we started out in the rain. Bummer.

We first headed out on I-20 East, goin' to Shreveport, which just happened to be Slick's home town. From Shreveport, we took an old highway down toward Baton Rouge,…where Bobby Magee was busted flat, wink, wink. That put us about 400 miles into the rain soaked trip so far, and it was fuckin' miserable shit, lemme assure you. From the Baton Rouge area we took I-12 East toward Mississippi. The rain had gone from a regular annoying drizzly rain in the beginning of the trip to a moderate rain, and now it had turned into sheets of monsoon rain blowing across the road.

We pushed on into the rain-soaked miserable night. It was getting hard to see. But at least Slick was doing OK back in his nice warm dry van, smokin' reefer and listenin' to tunes as we traveled down the soggy highway, hahaha. At one gas station they had those black plastic Hefty type trash bags, so we got them and made ourselves some really nice rainsuits. Maybe you've done it, too?

Ya pull out a nice big brand new fancy trash bag, unwind it in the rain and wind trying to keep it flat while you pull out your trusty Buck knife and cut a radiused hole in the center of the top for your head to poke through, then ya slice the top corners off so's your arms can stick through. There! Now put it on, you look just great. We got some smaller plastic trash bags to wear over our gloves. And that was it. Now we're good to go. Oh, and there was helmet laws where ever we rode on this trip, so we put on helmets too.

We stood there for a few seconds looking at each other, pointing and laughing our asses off at how goofy it was. So we kicked the bikes over and took off into the rain again. Now Harold and Stan and me didn't have front fenders on our girders, so we're getting the front wheel spray on top of the regular road rain shit. It was fuckin' miserable, gloomy and depressing, and we're supposed to be having fun? And before anyone thinks about putting the shop rag on your girder for a nice emergency front fender, we tried that shit and it was no good, totally useless.

We kept riding on, gettin' drenched in the rain, dark at night now. The sheets of rain kept blowin', and we kept ridin' on into the wet night. We were soooo fuckin' drenched down to the bone marrow, that if we had rode our bikes off a bridge down into a river and we sunk to the bottom of the river and sat down there on them for a fuckin' week, we couldn'ta been any wetter than we were right now. And then. it happened.

My Mikuni took the Big Shit. Its slide got stuck right where it was and would not budge. If I tried to roll the throttle on more… nuthin' happened. If I tried to roll it off to slow down…nuthin' happened. I banged on it with my right hand to see if I could loosen it up. Nope. It was stuck at the RPM that it was at, and the throttle cable had no control over it. That means going into turns or riding through the big water puddles on the highway, if Harold and Shelby slowed down, I'd nearly run into Harold. All I could do was hit the only brake I had, which was the old mechanical brake in back, and I could pull in the clutch lever, that was it. I was nearly helpless on a runaway chopper. And of course, when I pulled in the clutch lever, the engine went crazy on the RPMs. I was totally fucked…didn't know what to do.

I tried lookin' across over at Stan, trying to tell him and motion with my left hand what was going on, but it was no good. With all the racket from our bikes and the wind, he couldn't hear me. And with the sheets of rain coming down, he probably couldn't see me too good either. I was going into Panic Mode now…didn't know what to do.

Then up ahead through the drivin' rain I see one of them big ol' Shell gas station signs, the kind up really high with the big yellow squares with the red SHELL letters on 'em. An' holy shit, there was an exit ramp. So I made a panicked quick decision and wimped out and took that exit ramp. That's right, I chickened out and pulled away from our pack of bikes and hit the exit ramp for the Shell station. The rest of the guys kept going.

As I'm slowin' down to try and get under the Shell's roof over the gas pumps, the 74 AMF is still runnin' at its high RPMs, so I shut it off and coasted the rest of the way. I was disgusted with myself, with the 74 AMF Chopper, and especially the 44 mm Mikuni which had let me down. I felt like a total failure. I blew it. I banged on the Mikuni with my hand trying to knock the round slide down inside, cuz I figured it was stuck in the middle of its chamber. No use. Sigh. I'm now a quitter and I'm fucked.

Then maybe 40 steps away or so, there was a motel sitting back off the road a bit, and it had the 'VACANCY' neon sign lit up. In my rain-soaked addled state, I figured since I had already wimped out and blew it, I might as well go the rest of the way and be a Total Poser. Why not? So I went walking over to the motel office where the guy was still up with the lights on watching TV. I can only imagine what he musta thought about my soggy big ass covered in ripped up black plastic garbage bags come stalkin' into his office drippin' water on his floor, hahaha. He was probably thinking only a lunatic would be out riding a motorcycle on a night like this and he may've been right.

He had a room for me, so I flipped him the cash. He gave me the room key so I walked back outside into the rain over to where the 11 foot long 74 AMF Dead Chopper waited for me. It looked like it was staring at me with its one dead headlight eyeball, as if it was thinkin'…what the fuck you gonna do now?

I grabbed the drag bars, kicked in the kickstand and started pushing it over to the motel room. I felt lower than a snake's belly in a wagon rut. I felt like shit. Here were these guys who were heroes of mine, and they had invited me. yes, punk ass ME…to go ride with them on their road trip to Daytona, even though they had told me they never let guys as young as me ride with them, and now I saw why. I had let them down. I blew it. I was a total loser, even in my own eyes.

But I was also thinking to myself with a little pep talk, hey, I have ridden non-stop from Las Vegas to Amarillo before, and that was over 800 miles, so maybe I can catch up to them tomorrow? And if not, I'll surely meet them at the KOA Kampground in New Smyrna Beach, where the ABATE Chapters were camping and scheduled to meet in Daytona. We were some of the Dallas Texas Chapter of ABATE people. There is a chance I could still pull off this Daytona Run after all, if I could only get a decent break with the Mikuni.

And then I heard a distinct rumble from out of the rain storm.

I stopped right where I was, pushin' the dead 74 AMF Chopper kinda halfway between the gas station and motel, and just stood there in the pourin' rain holding onto the drag bars. The noise I heard had headlights that were vibratin' and jigglin' up and down, and behind those headlights was Slick's van. Holy shit. They actually came back to look for me?

The group of bikes pulls up right in front of me with the rain still pourin' down. Shelby sez "What's going on with you?" I thought he was sorta pissed off at me, and rightfully so. I told him "The carb took a shit on me and that's it for me tonight until I can get it all dried out." Then I said "I gotta motel room right there if you guys wanna crash. But if you guys wanna keep ridin', I can try to catch up with you tomorrow or I can meet you at the KOA Kampground in New Smyrna Beach."

Then while he's still sittin' on the Custom Panhead idlin' in the rain, Shelby sez "We really should get in some more miles tonight."

Then Stan sez, "Getting a motel room is the best thing I've heard all day. Fuck this rain!"

Then Shelby sez, "We really need to ride some more miles."

Next, Harold sez his magnificent words that I will remember to my dying day… "Shelby,…we know who we are. We don't hafta prove anything to anybody."

And the guys shut off their motors and started pulling their bikes up in front of the motel room. I wonder what the guy in the office thought? Slick parked his van over on the edge of the parking lot. We walked into the DRY motel room with a bit of relief. We threw our road bags down on the floor, got a few things out to let dry. We fired up some joints then Blue and Slick came in from the van with some beer for everyone. Then Shelby pushed the Show Pan into the motel room. I went into the bathroom and got a towel all

THE EARLY YEARS

nice and wet to wash the grime off Shelby's Tom-Bike, then I dried it with the other towels. Call it kissin' ass and tryin' to make up, or call it havin' respect for them for coming back for me.

All I know is that night meant more to me and was more important than any other night or day in my two wheeled life. Even when the 74 AMF Chopper eventually got its 6 page spread in Easyriders magazine, this stormy night right here meant more to me than that. And here's why. Cuz I blew it, I gave up, yet they came back for me, cuz they had accepted me as one of their own. Nothing ever made me feel prouder. I went from the depths of despair and embarrassment to the best feeling ever, all in less than a half hour.

We spent the rest of the night taking turns sleepin' in the two beds and sleepin/sittin' in the motel chairs while Blue and Slick slept out in the van. Tomorrow would be another day. And that tomorrow could be either better, or worse. even much much worse.

Here's another picture of Harold's Panhead Chopper, this time with the low-slung headlight.

PART 57: "THE EARLY YEARS"

More Misery Ridin' to Daytona 1977

The road side motel we crashed at the rainy night before was probably out around the border between Mississippi and Alabama, out around Biloxi and Mobile. So we had covered around 550 or 600 miles. in pouring rain. That means we had

about 300 or 350 miles or so to ride to Valdosta Georgia. That was our first destination, rather than riding directly into Daytona. Why? Cuz Shelby said so, that's why.

Well actually, that was the plan all along, cuz we wanted to ride in that Run to the Sun they did there every year that I had seen in the bike magazines back then, but had never been on myself…yet. For those unfamiliar with it, thousands and thousands of motorcycles of every type you can imagine converge on Valdosta. Then at the given time, High Noon or 3:00 PM or whatever it was, they all take off in one huge ass swarm riding into Daytona in one big two wheeled crowded mass headed down the highway. And that is still around a 200 mile ride. The deal is. we HAD to be in Valdosta in time to make that run, or it would be a Colossal Big Bummer for us.

So on this second morning of the trip, we woke up pretty early cuz we didn't really sleep all that much anyhow, just took turns trying to sleep in the two beds and chairs. I was feeling better this morning cuz during the night Shelby told me what was probably wrong with the Mikuni. He said it was water logged and the water made the slide stick in place and if I sprayed some WD-40 down in the throat, it would probably be OK. That made me feel good that it was an easy fix, and then made me feel kinda dumb for not thinking of it myself. Cuz my dad used to pull off the distributor caps on his old cars when they got wet or really humid and he'd spray WD-40 on the underside of the cap where the plugs fired, cuz the WD got rid of water and humidity. Why the hell didn't I think of that? I unscrewed the top chrome cap on the Mikuni, lifted it up with that big spring still attached to it and I sprayed the shit outta that throat and put it back together and guess what? It fired right up and the throttle worked again…yay.

We loaded up the gear on the bikes, pushed the Shelby Tom Show Pan out the door and loaded it up with the road gear and the skies had cleared and no rain in sight…yay again! Then we got gas at the station right next to us and ate breakfast. It was at this point that I realized how much longer it takes 6 people to eat and get gas than it does for 1 or 2 or 3 people like my previous bike trips, hah. Anyhow, we hit the road and took off to the east. All went fine for maybe two hours and the next gas stop. Then out on I-10 in southeastern Alabama, Blue's Knucklehead took a Big Shit. He had valve train issues. Bummer.

Our group was on the side of the road wondering what to do now. It had to go into Slick's van, no two ways about it. But the sidecar was full and heavy, so first we had to unload Blue's gear and the Harley Wing Plaques into the van. Then we had to detach the sidecar from the bike and load the side car up in the front of the van, then stick Blue Jay's Knuckle in beside Slick's Panhead. It was now a full van, no more room. Sounds like a fun morning, eh? It's a lot easier to talk about it than to do it, hahaha.

And now we're goin' down the highway again, headed to Valdosta. We kept riding with Shelby and Harold up front, Stan and me behind them, and Slick and Blue following us in Slick's van. We got us a caravan going now and it's still nice weather. We kept riding making good time and then later on we pulled in to get gas out around Bainbridge Georgia, maybe an hour and a half from Valdosta out there on Highway 84. And then when we got ready to leave? I kicked and kicked and kicked and kicked and no fire. The 74 AMF Chopper was dead as shit. Quick as I could, I pulled both spark plugs and put one back in the plug wire cap and held it up to the head and turned the kicker over, and…no luck. The plugs were not firing. No spark at all. Fuck.

And here at this stage is where it is handy to have a battery in your bike. Cuz without the battery, I had no juice. That was the deal with the Sebring Battery Eliminator, it worked fine,…as long as it worked. But if the bike won't run, then how can ya check to see where there ain't no spark? We didn't have time for this shit. And Slick's van was full, so now what? Brother Stan to the rescue.

Stan sez, "Fuck it. I got a rope, let's tie you on and I'll pull you there." I was like,… WHAT? Stan the Always Prepared Long Haul Trucker got out his nice fine mesh rope and tied it onto the back of his chopper, down at the area where the sissy bar meets the top of the fender. Then he walked back to me and gave me the loose end and showed me how to bring it through the risers and wrap it around the handlebar 3 times and then hold onto it. He said he'd done this lots of times before. Then Stan asked me "Do ya think you can hold onto this rope real good while we're going down the road?" I said "I guess I'll have to, and it can't be any worse than holding onto a bull rope, right?" Then Stan laughed some and then told me I'd hafta be our brakes, cuz if he tried to stop, I might ram into him. Gulp. Umm,… OK,… I guess?

He laughed and got back onto his Pan/Shovel Chopper, kicked it over, the other guys did, too, and off we went. So now Stan is pulling me with his rope to Valdosta Georgia, hahaha. And it was fuckin' cool. Kinda scary right at first, but I actually relaxed into it. It reminded me of the Coast Races Brudder Charles and Cuzzin Johnny and me had done up in the high mountains in Colorado two years before. It felt really weird and funny going that fast with no motor running. Stan was probably pulling me at 60 mph or so.

And all I could hear was Stan's pipes up in front of me and the wind blowing and my chain whirring through the sprockets, that was it.

By the time we got into Valdosta, the Official Start had already gone off, but it takes a loooong time for that many bikes to go through, so our group eventually got into the line up. But first, we had to make some fast changes. Slick wanted to ride his Panhead in the Run to the Sun and I don't think Stan was really crazy about pulling me in traffic, like bike traffic with a few crazies involved. Although if we needed him to, I bet Stan woulda pulled me all the way to Mexico City, haha. Anyhow in Valdosta we made the switch. We pulled Slick's Panhead out and stuck the busted 74 AMF Chopper in the van alongside Blue's busted Knucklehead.

THE EARLY YEARS

So now the group was still Shelby and Harold in front, and Stan and Slick riding behind them and now Blue is driving Slick's van with me riding shotgun. That means I was now the guy in charge of keeping the joints and music going in the Good Times Van. And then a weird thing happened. Slick started weaving his bike back and forth in his side of the lane, like a kid wobbling on a bicycle. Then he rode over kinda too close to Stan, and then Slick held his left hand out to Stan, palm side up, like he was sayin' Gimme Five or Gimme Some Skin, and Stan didn't feel like playing that game.

What Blue and me saw next was Stan's big boot come up and kick the shit outta Slick's fat bob gas tank, which made Slick wobble even more. Blue said "Holy shit, Slick nearly went down." And then I said "And if he woulda gone down, then you'da run over him with his own van" and Blue busted out laughing blowing out weed smoke at the same time and then we went into the laughing while coughing fits.

Well, our group finally made it into Daytona, and it took us forever to get through downtown cuz of all the bikes. But eventually we made it out to New Smyrna Beach to the KOA Kampground where all the other ABATE Chapters were camping. And we got into the Texas ABATE spots right next to the South Carolina ABATE Chapter.

SHOVELHEAD DAVE

So,…we made it. Yay! Now we gotta unload our bikes from Slick's van, set up camp, and figure out what is wrong with our sick motorsickles. And this photo here is the back side of one of the old timey T Shirts I wore on this run. That is the Harley dealer which cursed me with the 1974 AMF Shovelhead which I've ridden and loved since 1974,…a-hem.

Part 58: "The Early Years"

Made it to Daytona 1977

We woke up our first morning in the KOA Kampground in New Smyrna Beach with all the other ABATE Chapters. It was a nice and loud morning with all the bikes runnin' in and outta camp. I was very excited, but I'da been even more excited if the crappy flea bitten 74 AMF Chopper was runnin' and I could go ridin' with everybody else into town, hahaha.

Blue and me had gotten our busted bikes outta Slick's Good Times Van the night before and we set in to work right away this morning to see what was up with our busted machines. And speaking of Slick, he was now gone. Stan and him had gotten into some kinda beef the night before, Stan gave Slick a big haymaker to the whiskers, and Slick got pissed off and left our group. Didn't see Slick again until several weeks later back in Dallas. Since it wasn't none of my bid-ness, I never pried into what happened, so it remains a Daytona Mystery.

And now if I remember right, Blue knew some folks either in Daytona or some other town nearby and took his Knuckle in another van over to their shop to fix it. And I think it turned out to be a sucked valve that had gone down into the seat a bit too much, or maybe a broken valve spring? I ain't sure cuz I wasn't there, but do seem to remember that it was valve train related.

And Blue recently said it was a frozen valve guide. He had the head off by the time we got to the Suncapitol R & S. That first day he took Lou Kimzy's van to town to a guy's shop he knew, and pressed out that guide and was running that night. Blue went to town the next day and was standing next to Billy Tinney the photographer and got arrested for obstructing traffic for nothing. That's why he wasn't back in camp that night. An Outlaw that Blue knew bailed him out the next day and his Knuckle was still sitting on Main with a prospect watching it.

Meanwhile, I will say Daytona and New Smyrna had some really fantastic folks there cuz I saw many Good Samaritan Types haulin' busted outta state bikes in their Florida tagged pick up trucks. But right now, my Main Goal was to find out what happened to cause the flame-out with no spark in the shitty bowling ball Shovelhead. The day before, I had already checked the spark plugs at the gas station where it died, out there on the highway before we got into Valdosta so I already knew they were dead. Next, I was gonna start up the line of electrical components to see what I could find,…if anything.

So going back from the spark plugs the next item I was gonna check was the coil. I still had the stock 1974 coil cover on the bike, and that was the tight fitting chrome rectangular one. It is the type that has the single hex nut screw on the back side. So I pulled that screw out and pulled the cover off and set it on the ground next to me. And then I pulled the plugs out, put one plug back into the end of the spark plug cap, held it up against the head for ground, turned the key on, kicked the kicker through and guess what?

CRACKLE! A SPARK! So now what the fuck is going on? And just then Stan walked up and saw what I was up to. And then he saw the coil cover on the ground and he already knew what the problem was. He picked the cover up off the ground and laughed and said "You don't have an inner tube glued in here." I was like "what the fuck do you mean, hahaha?" Stan said "These coil covers fit too tight to the coil. You hit a big bump or wiggle them too much, they will touch the top or bottom post of your coil and short it out."

Well,…bust my britches, if that Stan didn't know his shit, eh? What an easy fix. Of course, I did not have any chunk of inner tube layin' around, but I did manage to get a little wad of paper with some electrical tape on both the top and bottom parts of the cover, put it back on, kicked it over and that wonderful trusty ol' 74 AMF Chopper that I love sooo much fired right up just like it was supposed to,…yay! I'm back in business again. Stan and me rode into Daytona with some of the others in our group of ABATE campers. And one of those other ABATE campers we rode into town with was a guy that Stan knew that was from his old home town of Spartanburg, South Carolina. I still remember the guy and his bike.

The guy's name was Possum and he rode an old Knucklehead Stroker, a 92 inch one. And what I remember best about Possum's Knuckle was the push rod covers. They were really different. When I asked him about the push rod covers, Possum said he had made them from VW Bug parts. So if any readers out there remember Possum, that was him and his Stroker Knuckle camping next to our ABATE group.

And also on this day, Blue, Shelby, Harold, Stan and me were riding into Daytona. And when we got to the edge of town, we stopped at a red light. Then all of a sudden these fuckin' cops came runnin' off the sidewalk and ran right up to us and started runnin' their billy clubs up our exhaust pipes, hahaha, how fuckin' rude, eh? And when the billy clubs didn't hit any mufflers, they told us to pull over to write us out tickets. So all of us had to pull over and then the cops didn't like the way we pulled over, so they yelled out "What the hell was that? A Chinese fire drill?" And then them pigs wrote us nice guys some tickets for no mufflers.

We rode on into town and started drinking beer and looking at the bikes and gals. Now THIS was Daytona Fun Time. What a party. We hit the famous and the infamous bike bars and got a coupla t shirts for souvenirs. Then we heard you didn't hafta wear helmets if you were ridin' on the beach. So we kicked the bikes over and rode over to the beach so's we could ride without them skid lids, see? So we're out there having fun, doing sandy burnouts, zig zaggin' back and forth spraying sand up everywhere, acting all crazy and shit. Then we rode back over to the sidewalk and got ready to ride back into the street, but first we had to put our brain buckets back on.

And when I was putting mine on, I found out what riding in the sand does to your bike. It gets sand ALL over the fucker,… groan. I had sand in the chain links, sand in the rear sprocket, sand in the countershaft sprocket, sand in the spoke nipples, and sand everywhere in between. So then we had to go find one of them coin car washes with the different bays and we pulled in and hosed our bikes off but good. And I ain't never ridden on a sandy beach since, hahaha. And here's another picture of Harold's Panhead Chopper, suicide clutch, true jockey shift, open belt drive. He was doing a little bit of paint touch up in this picture.

PART 59: "THE EARLY YEARS"

Uh-oh, Gawddammit, Daytona 1977

The third or fourth morning, can't remember for sure, but we were still camping at the KOA Kampground in New Smyrna Beach and we fired up the bikes to go into Daytona to eat, drink, and have us some fun times. We were doin' all the regular shit, eyeballing the gals and bikes, sneakin' in a puff or two when we could get away with it, and watchin' the asshole cops fuckin' with everybody. The Daytona goons had called in every cop department around, it seemed like, cuz there were shoulder patches from every surrounding town on the coppers' uniforms. After checkin' out a lot of the outrageous choppers, I decided to ride on back out to camp.

Our KOA was about a 15 minute ride down the beach from the main action in Daytona, so it was pretty close and convenient. Then while I was sittin' at a red light waitin' for the fucker to turn green, the fuckin' 74 AMF Chopper just up and died on me at the light. Kinda unusual. So while I'm there in the line of bikes and cars, I simply stood up from the seat and flipped the kicker pedal out with my right foot, then started to kick it down. Only problem was,… there was no compression. The kicker just fell through like it wasn't even hooked up to the tranny, hahaha. Oh cripes, what the fuck is wrong now?

The light turned green, the cars behind me started honkin', the bikes were swervin' around my dead ass which was now marooned in the middle of the street, so I jumped off and started pushing the 11 foot long chopper contraption over to the curb to get a better look of what was wrong. Could not see anything wrong. The open belt drive makes it easy to see the clutch rod, adjusting screw and lock nut, and they were all in place. The was no busted finger on the clutch hub, everything looked normal to me. Still,…no compression. Now I'm fucked, big time. All the guys I rode with were either back at camp or back in Daytona still partying.

Then, outta the wild blue yonder, here comes yet another one of them Good Samaritan Guys in his pick up truck with a couple of his buddies in back cuz they had been to town loading up on beer to take back to camp. They pulled over and told me they were also staying at the KOA and recognized my long chopper as being kinda close to their camp site. So they were also ABATE people, yay. They helped me load the fuckin' 74 AMF Shit Pile into the back of their truck and we hauled it back out to camp. This is becoming "Live to Haul, Haul to Live."

Back out at the KOA, we unloaded it and I pushed it over by my orange pup tent and parked it there in the dirt just like normal. Then I spied Shelby over there kinda wanderin' around talkin' to some other folks. I moseyed over and asked him if he could come over and see what he thought was up with the 74 Shit Chopper. Shelby comes over to look at it and I gave him the demonstration of how when I tried to kick it, there was no compression whatsoever, no resistance, the kicker just fell to the bottom.

Then Shelby looked at me with that dead pan Pat Paulsen expression from the Smothers Brothers TV show. He had a beer in one hand and his cigarette in the other. He took a swig of beer, then a drag on his smoke, blew it out, and then Shelby sez, "Dave,… I am a motorcycle mechanic. I work on motorcycles 50 weeks every year. I get only two weeks off each year to ride here and have some fun and relax. Guess what is the one thing I do not wanna do while I am on vacation?"

I nearly busted out laughing, but I held it in, then I said "Umm,…lemme guess? You do NOT wanna work on motorcycles while you are here on vacation?" He said "You got it. But tell you what, you pull off the nose cone cover and get it apart, then I'll come back over here and see what's wrong, then you can fix it."

Well, sheeit-dang, I couldn't ask for anything better than that, right? So I took the tool bag off the chopper, opened it up dumped all the tools out there in the dirt with me and started pulling shit apart. When I finally got the nose cone off, Shelby came back over and he sadly discovered that the little fuckin' key had busted out on the pinion shaft. Oh joy. The key is still there and so is the chunk of busted pinion shaft. There ain't no fixin' that shit in this dirt campground. And by this time, it was starting to get dark, which means there ain't gonna be no light to work with, plus it is gonna require a machine shop now and they'd all be closed. So that's it for this night. I'm fucked and got no runnin' wheels. And then the misery set in.

Since I'm grounded and can't do nuthin', I decided to just drown my many sorrows and get all fucked up stoned and drunk. Why not? Ain't nuthin' else to do. As the night wore on, I kept smokin' and drinkin' and gettin' more and more pissed off at that 74 AMF Piece of Shit Bowling Ball Bike. And I could no longer blame the 1974 Striking AMF Factory for the fuckups, cuz all these fuck ups are my doing. This 11 foot long fuckin' piece of shit Frankenstein Monster Chopper in front of me that's all broke down is MY own creation, can't blame nuthin' on anyone else. I built it, and now it don't run. I am fucked, fucked, fucked, and double fucked again.

Then suddenly from outta nowhere, Stan came riding in on his beautiful Pan/Shovel chopper and parked right next to me cuz our tents were neighbors. Stan asked what's up? I pointed at the broke down AMF Shit and said "That's what's up." And Stan saw the parts and tools in the dirt and got sorta interested in it, hahaha.

There was a nice campfire going by this time and we were standing next to it drinkin' beers and passin' a nice big fat joint back and forth. And I told Stan I had fuckin' had it with the AMF Shit. I confessed that I shoulda gotten a nice old Panhead or Knuckle all along, just like the guys told me I shoulda. I told Stan if I ever got the AMF Fucker running again, and after I rode it back home to Dallas, I was gonna sell the fuckin' sumbitch to the first unlucky moron bastard that wanted it, bwahahaha. I hated it, hated it, hated it. Gawddamn I hate that 74 AMF Shit Bike.

Then Stan told me to simmer down and he started talking to me. I guess this was what you'd call my first "Brother to Brother Talk" right there that night around the campfire at Daytona Bike Week.

He told me shit like all motors are mechanical things and they all will have problems from time to time. I said well this is the THIRD time this fucker has crapped out on me on this trip and it ain't even half over yet, hahaha. Stan said that's the luck of the draw. It could happen to anybody. It just happened to be my bike right at this moment in time. That didn't make me feel any better.

So Stan kept on talking, trying to explain things and get them into perspective and then get the information embedded into my half empty drunken noggin. I told him that I liked his and Harold's frames better than mine, cuz mine was a 1971 D&D Jammer that I got already used, and I said I liked those old Harley rigid frames better than mine. Stan countered with this line,…well any rigid Harley is gonna be at least 20 years old now. Your frame is newer metal and it's lighter weight for better handling. Plus it's already got the rake and stretch in it so you don't hafta go through all that work. When I told Stan that I like the looks of the generator motors' lower ends better than the cone Shovels, he said,…he agreed.

And then he started in talking about performance. He told me how the Shovel heads work better, they run cooler and breathe and flow air better than the older styles. He told me since I already had Shelby stroke the motor, that the hardest part was already over, and then he said there is all kinds of untapped power in the cone Shovel motors. Then he told me to stick with what I got. Make it better and better as time goes by. And that particular night around that particular campfire was the night I decided to stick with that fuckin' 74 AMF Piece of Shit forever, for better or worse, til death do us part. So here we are now, 45 years later, it's been through 4 motor and tranny builds, 7 bare frame up builds, cut the frame neck twice, and I'm still ridin' it and still rebuildin' on it, and still changin' it around for new looks every so often. So I guess Stan's Talk took effect. I finally got it. Tomorrow at the KOA Kampground will be a new day and things might get better,…maybe? And maybe not.

We had a pretty big campfire or bonfire going and someone threw a palm tree trunk in there and it caught on fire good. Then some wasted guy came along and laid down on the tree and passed

THE EARLY YEARS

out. His head was about 4 feet from the fire and the guys were betting if the fire would get to him before the sun came up.

Blue said what happens if he wakes up and gets up? So to prevent that from happening, they tied him to the tree trunk and then he woke up screamin' around 7:30 that evening.

And then these are Blue's words: "I cranked up my Knuckle and was going to ride around the fire to my tent but I accidentally slammed it into R and popped the foot clutch and went right through the fire backwards with both feet on the floorboards.

Stopped right next to my tent turned it off, put down the kickstand and acted like it was nothing. Turned and looked at the fire and guys were pouring out their beers and threw their joint in the fire."

This is Blue on the far left side sittin' on his Red Knuckle, Stan is right next to him, then another guy from Spartanburg who we don't remember his name, but he was a friend of Possum's,…and that is Possum over on the far right side working on his Knuckle stroker.

And this photo here is the only other photo I have of Stan. That's him on the right and me on the left and Shelby took the picture. WHAT? Shelby had a camera? I guess so, cuz he's the one that took it and then gave it to me later.

SHOVELHEAD DAVE

Part 60: "The Early Years"

Holy Shit! Daytona 1977

Woke up in the tent the next morning and had a nice little project to do. And it was called,…get the 74 AMF Chopper running again. Our ABATE camping neighbors once again played Good Samaritan and hauled my crummy chopper to town to a machine shop somebody (maybe Blue?) knew about.

We unloaded the 11 foot long monster and got it into the shop where the machinist expertly put the key back in and filled the busted out hole in the pinion shaft like a good Doc Holiday dentist would do. Then he got his little high speed air grinder and ground the filling down nice and smooth until it was good as new. Paid the nice guy for his excellent work, then we loaded it back up, hauled it back to camp, then unloaded it again. My back is gettin' a little bit sore just thinking about all this heavy chopper liftin' shit, hahaha.

OK now it's time to put the fucker back together so's I can have a runnin' bike again like all the big kids got and go have some Daytona Fun instead of being broke down here in the dirt. Only problem was, I could not reassemble it just yet, cuz there were little bronze grindings/shavings everywhere. I did not have an air hose, no cans of compressed air, no Brak-Kleen, no nuthin'. So I did the only thing I could think of. Due to all the boozers in camp, there were dozens of empty beer cans all over the place so I grabbed one for a volunteer and cut off the top with my Buck knife and wiped the can out nice and clean with my dirty red shop rag. Then I disconnected the fuel line on the petcock and drained some gas into the beer can.

And now I'm down in the dirt on my knees, holding the frame of the chopper with my left hand, leanin' it over toward me, while the beer can is in my right hand and I'm dousin' the gas up into the nose cone area to clean out the grinder shavings, see? I doused it with the gas, then stood the bike back up, drained some more gas into the can, leaned the bike over, doused it 3 or 4 times, then stood it back up. Third time's the charm, right?

So on the third time, I leaned the bike over with my left hand again, started dousing out the shavings with the gas again, when I heard some popping firecrackers going off behind me, hahaha. Somebody had lit up one of them strings of 100 firecrackers, and I'm sittin' there in the big puddle of gas in the dirt? See where this is going now? I'm thinkin' to myself, 'I hope none of them firecrackers come poppin' over this way by me'…when…

BANG-POP… WHOOSH! Immediately, this big fire ball comes up from the ground, and shoots up by me on each side of my head. Through reflex, I closed my eyes and let go of the chopper with my left hand and threw both my arms up around my punkin haid to protect it from the fire ball. And then I thought,… "OH SHIT! THE BIKE!" And I opened my eyeballs just in time to see the flames licking up through the cylinders and heads,…this action is NOT good.

I panicked and reached down and grabbed the chopper frame right behind the gas tank with both hands and I fuckin' threw that sumbitch a good 4 or 5 feet away, I shit ya not, it flipped like a fish outta water. I was like one of them little ol' grannies lifting up her car to save her trapped one-eyed and three-legged alley cat. I stepped back and let the fire burn out, while the chopper was over on its side a few safe feet away. And looking back now, I wonder what woulda happened if the firecracker had gone off while I still had the petcock open? Imagine the gas on the ground catching on fire, and then going up the stream of gas until it hit the open petcock? See there? Things can always be worse.

And there was also a really funny thing that happened that Blue reminded me about. There was this big dog that was running around barking at everyone in the campground, just wouldn't shut up. And some 1% guys locked it in a van. They had a 55 gallon stew going on the fire. They shaved the dog and put the hair on top of the stew.

When the guy came by, they said they hadn't seen his dog but they offered him a bowl and when he saw the hair he about died, hahaha. They gave the dog back the next day.

And for the happy part, I finally got the 74 AMF fucker back together out there in the campground dirt. It was kicking over and running good again. And this photo here is my Daytona Patch.

PART 61: "THE EARLY YEARS"

Crunchin' Metal & Sparks Daytona 1977

They say all good things must come to an end and thankfully,...so must the bad things,...eventually,...hopefully. And you'd think there had been enough bad things happening to us on this trip that they'd be over by now. But. they weren't. You'd think we had used up our fair share of bad luck. But. we hadn't.

The 74 AMF Chopper had the carb trouble in the monsoon, then the electrical trouble on the way to Valdosta, the key breaking outta the pinion shaft, and Blue's Knuckle had its valve issue and Blue himself had been thrown in The Can by the fuckin' Daytona Pigs for "obstructing traffic" which translates to regular English as standing in the street while Billy Tinney was taking some pictures of bikes and babes.

On the bright side, the Shelby/Tom Show Pan took Fourth Place in the Rat's Hole Show and won Most Unusual, so that was good. And Shelby's and Harold's and Stan's motorsickles all did good with no issues that I remember and none of them got thrown in jail, so that was good. And it was one helluva fun party for sure. I had a blast there in spite of everything else that took a Big Shit on me.

But now? Now it's getting to be that time for Blue and me to ride back to Dallas. We had jobs to get back to. Shelby, Harold and Stan had 2 weeks for their fun, but Blue and me didn't have that much time. So we were gonna ride back by ourselves. We said our goodbyes to the new friends we'd met in the KOA Kampground and knew we'd be seeing the rest of our ABATE group pretty soon once we all got back home, and especially Blue would cuz he was President of ABATE in Dallas.

Blue's trusty Knuckle was down to two wheels now cuz he was without the sidecar. I don't remember if he left it with friends or sold it to somebody there? All I remember is he was now on two wheels instead of three. So Blue kicked over his Knuckle and I kicked over the 74 AMF and it even started,…wow. So off we took. From Daytona we rode up a little bit north in Florida until we turned left and headed west along the Florida Panhandle above the Gulf. The distance from Daytona back to Dallas was about 1,100 miles,…just like it had been 1,100 from Dallas to Daytona. "That's a joke son, that's a joke." -Foghorn Leghorn

We rode on through the Florida Panhandle, sneakin' underneath Alabama by the Gulf and by Pensacola. We crossed into Alabama and made it through Mobile. By the time we got through Mobile it had been dark for quite a while cuz we had now covered around 500 miles already and had been on the road for 10 or 11 hours. I think it mighta been Stan the Trucker that gave us some of those little trucker helpers to help us along our two wheeled journey through the midnight hours, but I ain't swearin' to it. All I know is we wound up riding up by Hattiesburg around midnight or later, and Hattiesburg is up a little bit further north into the bottom of Mississippi.

And it was out there by Hattiesburg where everything went to Total Shit. Blue's tail light bulb had burned out a coupla hours before, so he ain't got no tail light now. I had a spare tail light bulb, but my electrical system is 12 volt while Blue's Knuckle is 6 volt. In an effort to fool the cops from pullin' us over, Blue was riding a bit in front of me, cuz I had my tail light still working plus I had a running light down on the side. So we were hopin' if a cop saw two bikes go ridin' by, and he looked at the back ends as we rode by, he'd still see two lights in the back of us instead of just the one,…see? Cops can be easily fooled at certain times, wink, wink.

The highway we were on came to a "T" intersection. There was a truck stop with some lights a bit off to our right hand side, other than that, it was pitch black out there in the dark boonies. As we were gettin' ready to turn right on the highway, I yelled out to ask Blue if he wanted to pull into the truck stop for some coffee or anything to eat. Then I saw Blue's Knuckle pull away and I thought either he didn't hear me or maybe he didn't want anything right then. I watched him disappearing into the dark night, and since his tail light was out, I didn't see where he was going. So I started up kinda fast to go catch up with him.

I wound off 1st gear, shifted into 2nd, wound it out and just as I was gonna shift into 3rd gear,...there was Blue. He had apparently heard me, had gone up the road a bit, then was turning right to go into the truck stop lot. But,...it was too late. What I remember is my head light shinin' on Blue's Red Knuckle in the darkness as the long girder rammed right into his bike, catching him smack dab in the middle, at the neck of his frame. Oh shit.

The impact knocked Blue and his Knuckle to the ground, metal grindin' and scrapin' and sparks flyin' out in the middle of nowhere. Meanwhile, I'm flyin' like a bird goin' over the top of Blue's Knuckle and I remember seeing the long chopper going upside down with stars below me and black ground on top. Kinda weird, but that's what I saw. Then once both our motors died, all got Quiet on the Southern Front. I remember yelling out to Blue to see if he was OK. I heard him yell back. I was over in the gravel on the side of the road a few feet from the AMF Chop. I heard Blue yell out again and when I got up and tried to walk to where he was, I collapsed in the road cuz my left foot was broke and would not step. So I crawled in the gravel on my hands and bloody knees some.

And then? And then, outta nowhere, just a few seconds later here's the cops. I don't remember if they were State Patrol or County Sheriffs, all I remember is they were there. They musta been eatin' in the truck stop to get there that fast. I had on a T shirt that had a front pocket on it, remember them? And in that front pocket was a few hand rolled ciggie-butts, if ya know what I mean. And we are in Mississippi...with weed...in 1977. Ooops. Gulp.

The cops are asking questions and I reached into the T shirt pocket and pulled out the joints and tried to hide and crumble them in my hand as best as I could and then flung 'em out toward the weeds on the side of the road while the cops were not looking. While Blue's fine ol' Knuckle was all fucked up, at least he could still walk around. The cops called the ambulance.

Now I'm gonna relay this sordid tale from Blue's view,... "I was ridin' along on my beautiful Knucklehead having fun enjoying a good buzz in Hattiesburg Mississippi one fine night when this 22 year old punk kid on a kooky dangerous 11 foot long chopper came along and ran right into me. He fuckin' T-Boned me doing about 45 or 50 miles per hour with no warning whatsoever."

The ambulance came. Blue stayed there talking with the cops and musta made some arrangements for the bikes to be kept in the truck stop or a nearby garage cuz neither one would run. As for me? They loaded my greezy ass into the ambulance and we took off to the hospital. There was the one guy driving it, and then the other guy got in the back with me, taking my blood pressure and heart beat, and other high toned expensive hoidy toidy medical shit like that.

When he was done, I folded my arms across my chest. And when I did that, guess what the fuck happened next? I'll tell ya. When I folded my right arm across my chest, my right hand landed on the T shirt pocket and can ya guess what was still in it? If you guessed one big fat joint was still left in there, then you just won some kinda prize, but don't ask me what kinda prize cuz I ain't got no clue. Gulp. Mississippi...weed,...1977.

So now I'm kinda in an even bigger panic, hahaha. What the hell am I gonna do with that nice big fat joint? Would the doctors wanna smoke it before they operate on me? Probably not, hahaha. And once they get me into the hospital, I am their meat then. They are gonna take all my clothes off, leavin' me all nekked an' shit and then they're gonna bust me when they find that joint in that pocket. I had to think fast. We were gettin' closer to the hospital; I could tell by the radio communication and what the two ambulance guys were sayin' to each other.

When we got there, they shut off the siren and we started to back into the loading dock where they unload the greezy chopper guys, right next to the dumpster, I'm sure. And when the guy next to me got up to open the back door of the ambulance... THEN,... I made my move and grabbed that gawd awful tastin' joint and gobbled it up while they weren't lookin'. Talk about nastiness,...yuck. It was like having severe cotton mouth and somebody gives you some dirt and hay to eat. Yum. So, they wheeled me into the Emergency Room and got me ready for surgery. I asked them if I could PLEEZE have some water and they said nope, you are in shock and you are going into surgery, you can't have anything to drink. Bummer.

And here is Blue's version he recently mentioned: "I remember it like yesterday. Smack I was down. Shut off the motor and got to you. Kept the cop, state Po Po busy while they were loading you up. The officer helped me push your bike across the road to a gas station/U Haul place. Then I kicked my fender straight, fired up my bike and started across the road. The owner said he would store our bikes for one week in a moving truck. He opened the back and pulled out the ramp. I hit it hard on the bike all the way to the front of the cab. Took me, the owner, the Po Po, and a mechanic from the truck stop to push yours up in there. Took care of business and they locked it up with my buds and gun in my sleeping bag. Cop took me to the hospital. They said they were taking care of you. Told them my chest hurt a little so they x-rayed me, 6 broke ribs on the left side where your bike hit me. They wanted to put me in the hospital. I said just tape it up, I've got to go, little helpers were kicking good.

They made me sign a form to find them not in fault if my lung started bleeding. Cop took me to the bus station. I never forget what he said 'go home, get something to get your bikes, then go back to Texas, you don't belong in this state.' Long painful ride home and in 48 hours I was back."

This is the 11 foot long 74 AMF Chopper safe at home before I left on this gawd-awful funny cursed road trip, hahaha, sniff, sniff. And that is my buddy Mike's Chevy Panel Job and my buddy Gary's 1975 Black Sportster, the one that rode between Brudder Charles and me doin' a hunnerd and busted the 74 AMF's clutch lever off.

THE EARLY YEARS

PART 62: "THE EARLY YEARS"

Busted Foot in Hattiesburg 1977

Once the ambulance hauled my stinky butt into the hospital they started asking all kinds of dumb questions, like,…did I have a job, who was my insurance, all that kinda boring shit. I said yes I got a fuckin' job, that's why I was in a hurry to get back to Dallas, to go back to work, hahaha. They also told me that my left foot was soooo smashed up that they were probably gonna cut my three little piggy toes off. I told them I ain't signin' nuthin' to allow them to cut anything off, if they couldn't fix me up to get me back to Dallas somehow, like in a jet powered helicopter or a fancy private jet with booze would be just fine, thank you.

I remember Blue comin' in and he was smashed up, too, like he had been in a motorsickle wreck. He wound up with 6 busted ribs, and even with the busted ribs pain, he still managed to get our bikes stashed in a safe place for 7 days and then he took off back to Dallas.

And then they wheeled me into the operating room and another gal came out and shot me up with the Good Juice, told me to count backwards from 10 and I think I got to about 7. That stuff just plain overruled the trucker helpers and weed in my system, like it was Total Shut Down, hah. So I went out like a light.

Zzzzzzzzzzzzzzzzzzzzzzzzz………………………

The next thing that happened was a loud snoring noise in my face. I opened my eyes just in time to see this huge dork on a gurney next to me just sawin' logs like they was juicy hamburgers.

I called out to nobody in particular… "Where in the hell am I? In the recovery room?" A purdy little Mississippi gal drawled "Ah've bin waitin' fer yew ta say somethin' like that" and she wheeled me into my own fancy private hospital room, no room mates. Good. I didn't feel like talkin' to nobody anyhow.

I'm from Dixie Land myself, but I ain't gonna cotton to these Mississippi guy-goons and kiss their rusty butts cuz they weren't very friendly folks,...not friendly like us nice Texans are. The gals seemed to be OK, but not the guys. And if any guys from Mississippi are reading this, you can tell your fuckin' cops to lighten up a bit, OK? They gave Blue exactly 7 days to get our bikes and get outta their state, for real.

Anyhow, now they had my foot all wrapped up and elevated, and the wrapping was as big as a basketball. It hurt like hell. I used the phone in my Luxury Suite and called my folks back home and told them I was in a hospital out in Mississippi of all places. They reacted exactly like I figured they would. My dad got kinda pissed off like 'I told you them motorsickles are bad', and my poor mom started cryin' over the phone. I had to settle them both down.

I said something like this to them "Look, it's just a busted foot. I ain't dead and my leg ain't cut off. I'm still alive and kickin'. I will be OK. Pretend I broke my foot playing football or riding bulls then it won't seem so bad." That seemed to settle them down a little bit. OK, that takes care of business, now I can try to relax a bit,...except the foot is throbbing like crazy. More pain shots please. Sorry, you can't have one yet. That type of shit.

So the first day I slept most of the time and that was OK cuz I hadn't got much sleep in Daytona cuz I was busy tryin' to have fun,...workin' on the 74 AMF Chopper in the dirt, hah. The next day I remember after I et up the breakfast they brought in on the tray, the doc and nurse gal unwrapped my left foot so's I could take a nice gander at it. I nearly threw up.

I could not believe that big ass bloody and black and purple swollen football on the end of my leg was actually my foot, and it had two big incisions going down the top of it where they had been cutting it all up having fun, with these Frankenstein type big black fishing line stiches on it. I bet they were telling Texas Aggie jokes while they did it. Then they told me how fucked up it was. And they said there was no way they could put a cast on it until the swelling went down. They said that could be a few days.

Hmm. So I'm stuck there now for a bit. Later in the day, this really purdy little gal came in to visit me. I was shocked!

Like,…really? You are an angel sent here to visit,… ME? Are you sure you are in the right room? She said my name and said yes, she was here in the right room to visit me. So she asked me all kinds of usual questions, like where you from, what you been doing, shit like that. I think she wasn't expecting the answers she got from me. "Oh man, I've been raisin' hell down at Daytona Bike Week on my Chopped Hawg for the past few days and man, we been partying' our butts off, you would not believe all the shit going on there." She left after a little bit longer. I found out later from the nurse that the gal was a hospital employee who got paid to visit friendless bums like me who had no family there.

I snoozed some more. And then? What happened the next day?

I was a-layin' there watching some stupid day time TV. When suddenly…the door cracked open. And then?

And then, Blue poked his head into the room, hahaha! And what else happened? His lady Lucious Linda was there with him! I asked "What are you guys doing here?" Blue sez, "Where are your clothes?" I pointed to the little cabinet over in the corner and said "Right in there." And then Blue grabbed a wheel chair and Linda grabbed the (dirty filthy) greezies and I slid over into the wheel chair and Linda put the clothes in my lap, and grabbed the cheap-o crutches the nurses had given me. I'm still naked wearing that flimsy see-through hospital gown that's open in the back where your butt hangs out, like I'm some ol' floozie that worked for Miss Kitty at the Longbranch Saloon in Dodge City, hahaha. And then?

And then Blue and Linda started wheelin' me outta the hospital, bwahaha. That's right, they were pushin' me right down the hallway while the docs and nurses yelled out for us to stop, we can't go yet, you aren't supposed to be leaving, that kinda shit.

They kept pushin' me right passed the front reception desk and then out the front door and there was Tom's beautiful ol' lady sittin' in their idlin' fancy painted van, waiting to make the mad dash perfect getaway.

Blue had been very busy, even with his half dozen busted ribs. He had both our bikes on a trailer hitched up to the van and I slid

THE EARLY YEARS

over into the back of the van where they had a nice mattress laid out for me, with tunes playing yet. Then Blue Jay shoved the wheel chair outta the way and next thing ya know, 3 van doors slammed shut and off we took, gettin' the hell outta Mississippi. Next thing I knew I smelt the sweet smell of Tom's Fine Weed and off we went down the road with music playin'. I think my dang foot even quit hurtin' for just a little bit. Next stop? Dallas. 500 miles away.

This picture here is rather ironic, eh? This is my Daytona 1977 souvenir ashtray from the KOA Kampground office. I, umm,…kinda borrowed it to remember the place by. Ya know? Like,… Florida? Fun in the sun and sand? Then I got a broken foot outta the deal, hahaha? And this ashtray was in my duffelbag and if ya look really close, you can see where it got busted in the crash and I had to glue it back together in order to put my joints and roaches in it all these years later. It's busted and then glued right across the heel part. And it is a right foot while it was my left foot that got busted. And if this ashtray woulda been the left foot and if it had broken across the middle of the foot and toes, then I'da felt really creepy. I ain't all that superstitious, I'm just a little bit 'stitious.

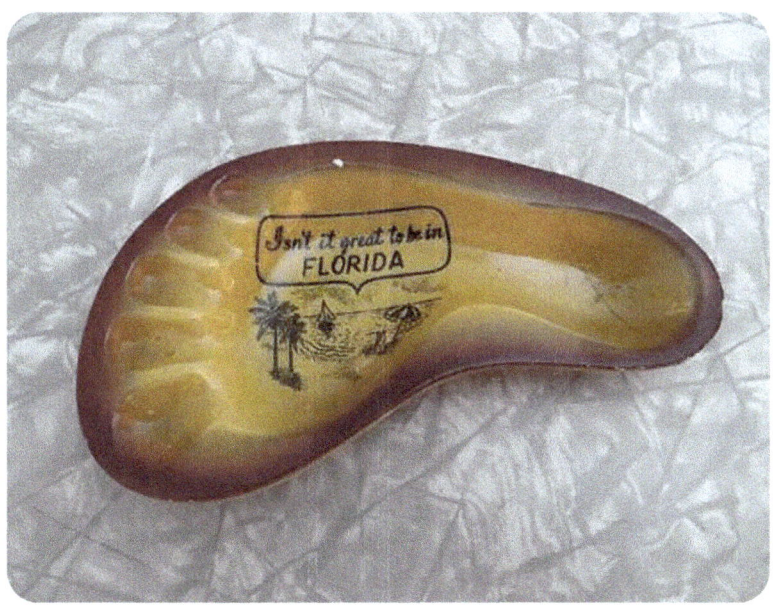

PART 63: "THE EARLY YEARS"

Back in Dallas 1977

Blue and his nice lady Luscious Linda and Brother Speed Tom's lady (I think her name was Sandy, or Cindy, or Candy? but ain't sure) got us back to Dallas in the nice fancy custom van all in one piece. Blue dumped me and the 11 foot long 74 AMF Chopper off at my crackerbox house and then went to unload and fix his beautiful ol' Red Knucklehead. If I remember right, I think Blue said I cracked his Knuckle's frame in 3 different places,…yikes. Plus his 6 busted ribs. Ouch.

And then all of a sudden, 'Realness on the Financial Front' set in, hah. Like,… OK, there Mister Smarty Pants, what the hell are ya gonna do for money now? I ain't got no printin' press, bummer. And I got a busted foot still too swollen to go into a cast, the bike is kinda busted up but turned out to be not too bad, more about that later. But the main thing I was worried about was CASH. I had taken most of my loot with me to Daytona and had blown it having fun and breaking down and payin' a stoo-pid fuckin' ticket in Daytona for loud pipes. And since I had not been 'laid off due to lack of work' and was now unable to do construction work right that minute, that meant I was not eligible for unemployment checks. Bummer. Plus I still had carpenter apprentice school to get to, and that was 2 nights a week while I still worked full time before the crash.

And since I had not been hurt on the job, that meant I could not get workers' compensation. Hmm. I got a house payment due coming up soon. After a coupla days somebody told me about a system for the poor folks that would either totally pay or help pay the rents in times such as this. That sounded good. So I hobbled down there with my brudder driving in his car, a 1970 Mach 1 Mustang, that

THE EARLY YEARS

Pumpkin Orange color trimmed in Black with the Shaker Hood. But when I talked to those folks, they said nope, no dice. If I had been a renter, they'd help me. But since I was buyin' my own house, forget about it. No help.

I asked why not help me, a usually hard workin' construction worker and tax payer down on his luck? They said they would not help some guy like me pay on his house. I countered with why not? They said cuz that is adding to your net wealth since you are not a renter. I came back with so, you are adding to landlords' net wealth, what about that? Silence. On the way out, I reminded them it's us taxpayers that make their paychecks possible. Next out of total desperation, I swallowed what was left of my pride and went to get food stamps. Nope, she said I made too much money the year before to get them, hahaha. Dang, folks, it's gettin' tough out there.

So 'The Man's System' forced me to do the only thing left that I could possibly do to get by. Try to sell weed. Now maybe or maybe not I got LBs for 90 bucks, and maybe or maybe not I sold lids for 10 bucks and maybe or maybe not I made 70 bucks off each pound. And maybe or maybe not I sold 4 or 5 LBs a month. I had different friends that worked all 3 shifts, so maybe or maybe not I was camped out on my living room couch with the Technics stereo playin' with my left leg up on another chair and maybe or maybe not I could see who was or was not at the door in case they did or did not want some weed for maybe or maybe not 10 bucks a lid.

Meanwhile, on the Foot Front, I got a nice set of wooden crutches with the rubber underarm pads on them and the rubber boot on the bottom, and my regular doc told me about this foot specialist over in Arlington, a goon named Dr. Vasshole. There, I kinda said his name…cuz we probably shouldn't really use it, his family is wealthy and will sue, hahaha. I mean, bwahaha! so ha-ha-ha, you fuckin' Dr. Fucker. My brudder drove me over to see this doc for the first time. Although I had two cars, the 68 Mustang and the 63 Rat Sting Ray, I couldn't drive either one cuz of my busted up left foot not being able to work a car's clutch pedal, see? So the 74 AMF Chopper is all the transportation I have that I can actually ride,… hopefully. But first I had to get the swelling down so I could get into a cast and I had to get the 74 AMF Chopper up and running again,…with one good foot.

Well, on my first visit to see this professional saw bones, he asked me how did the busted foot happen. I told him I had a motorcycle wreck in Mississippi. I'll never forget, he sez, "Ahh,…a murder cycle wreck." I said "So you don't like bikes, huh?" He sez, "Oh no. Just the opposite. I love them. They are one of my main sources of income" and he starts laughing, hahaha. I shoulda walked out right then and found another doc, but I was 22 years old and…well…you know. Then he took some X-Rays of my foot, and came in laughing about them. When I asked "What's so funny?" He said "Your X-Rays. I guess that's the way they fix things in Mississippi." So my foot was still fucked up. Hmm. Then he told me to come back in 3 more days and said he'd probably put it in a cast then. OK, sounds good. Go back home.

Meanwhile I got some good friends and neighbors bringing food by, like Ray and Debra who lived up the street and rode a Black 1972 Super Glide. I also had a Bob's Burgers down at the end of my block so I lived on them nicer tasty burgers for a while, too. And then one day my folks came over unexpectedly to visit and 'help out' around the house.

And while I was kinda snoozin' on the couch, my dear ol' mom did something really drastic. She washed my greezy jeans! Oh noooooooo! They were my favorite riding Levis, oil soaked and water repellent and could probably stand up in the corner by themselves, hah. And they had gotten ripped to shreds in the wreck in Hattiesburg, plus the Hattiesburg emergency room docs had to cut them off me, so now they were not only oil soaked, they were also ripped and sliced, and covered in my dark red dried blood. In other words, they looked really cool and made a great fuckin' souvenir that money could not buy. And my mom thought they were just regular garden variety dirty ol' Levis that needed washing, so she ruined them. Sigh.

And yes, I still have them, but they don't look the same, sniff, sniff.

Meanwhile, on the 74 AMF Chopper front. Although the 74 AMF looked kinda beat up now, it did before the wreck anyhow, wink, wink. The main damage in the crash was knocking the 44 mm Mikuni off its Jerry Branch intake, which had a rubber mount anyhow so that was no biggie, just stuck it back on and got a new throttle cable. The headlight bulb was busted, so I got a new bulb for $3.95 or whatever they cost-ted back then at Napa. And the worst part was the impact broke the bung/mounting spot on the girder for the shock to mount on. The bottom of the shock on the girder was now hanglin' loose, kinda blowin' in the wind type of deal. So I had to hook the girder up rigid now in order to keep riding it, since it is my only wheels I got that I can actually ride.

Rigid frame + rigid girder + busted foot + bumps = more pain. Three days later I rode in my brudder's car one last time to the foot doc and he finally got me into a cast from my calf down to my toes, with the toes hangin' out the open front. And now the swollen ends of my foot has gone down, but it is still black and purple and there were 3 stainless steel pins hangin' out the fronts of all three little toes-ses. It looked really cool, got me lots of sympathy in the grocery stores and beer barns, shit like that. People signed it, too. And with the bike back together and the foot in a cast, NOW I can finally get around on my own. How?

Simple. I'd strap each crutch on each side of the girder with bungee cords, one across the top that caught both crutches, and one across the bottom that caught the ends. Then I had one more bungee that I hooked onto the top bungee and brought it up over the handlebar risers and back down to the same bungee, ropin' it in, see? So that kept the crutches up and prevented them from slidin' down toward the front Invader 5 Spoke wheel. Don't want no crutches gettin' involved with no rollin' front wheel.

I also got the hobblin' routine down pretty good. I'd hobble out to the chopper on the crutches, stand on my good foot while I tied them onto the girder, then I'd hobble back to the carb side of the chop and put my left knee on the seat and kick the sucker over like normal with my good foot and hope like hell that the kick stand did not fold up, hardy har har. When it fired up, then I'd hop down in the seat and hang the foot cast out over the #1 steel footpeg. I'd let the entire foot hang over the peg. And that way I could shift the shifter peg up and down with the back heel of the cast, get it?

These pictures here are of Blue's Harley Wings Plaque that he cast himself. He used to sell these in the back page ads of Easyriders magazines. I got this one from Blue at Daytona and hauled it all the way back home, hahaha. It was in the duffelbag and also went through the wreck. You can see its road rash on the top left corner where it scraped through the bag and ground itself on the road. Cool, eh? That makes it worth more to those collectors on the stupid TV shows, haha. After moving through 4 states over the past 42 years, the original little brass Daytona 1977 tag on the bottom finally fell off somewhere, so I had another one made and this time I drilled 2 holes in it and nailed the fucker on there so it ain't comin' off ever again.

PART 64: "THE EARLY YEARS"

Dr. Vasshole, April 1977

So, once I got my new kick starting routine down for kickin' the Shovelhead over, it became less of a burden to go places. People stared at me and laughed some, but so what? At least I was ridin' my bike again, and they weren't.

After several more days went by, it was time to strap them crutches on the +25" over flame cut girder and go see that so-called foot specialist, the Dr. Vasshole. I got to really hate that fuckin' prick. What an obnoxious arrogant goon he was. You could tell in 2 minutes that he was raised as a spoiled rich brat who now treated his own staff like slaves or runaway stray dogs with rabies.

And he was a fuckin' tennis freak. He just LOVED everything about tennis. He had tennis related pictures hanging on his walls in the office, like Jimmy Connors and John McEnroe shit. Dr. Asshole V, traveled to places like Boston and Los Angeles to see the professional tennis matches. He belonged to his own tennis club and played alla time. I'm telling this shit cuz it has to do with the story in a bit.

So on this day I rode the chopper over to his office, which sat on the ground floor in a medical complex in Arlington Texas, with glass windows all around. That means he was able to see me ride up on the "muder-cycle" see? I pulled in, shut the Shovelhead off, grabbed my crutches and hobbled into the building and told the receptionist here I am, yay. Eventually they put me in a room. I was on one of those tables like you've seen before, the kind that raises up on one end and it's covered in the white paper they rip up when you leave so they can put down new white paper for their next victim. The cast on my foot was full plaster out to the front on the bottom side, but not on top.

The top side came back about halfway up my foot to where all the stitches showed and could be exposed to the air, I guess?

And I'm sittin' on that table with my legs out in front of me when The Supreme Asshole walks in. He asked me how I'm doing, oh just fine and dandy. Then he sez, "I see you rode your murder-cycle in today. If my foot looked like yours because of a muder- cycle, I would never ride it again." I said "Oh really? Well what if you were playing tennis and you went to jump over the net at the end of your match? And what if your foot got caught on the net and tripped you and you fell and broke your wrist? Would you never play tennis again?" He said "That's different. Tennis is a sport." I said "It's the same damn thing. We both like what we like. If what I like sometimes hurts me, I work around it, I don't quit." He ignored me after that one. Wonder why? Smart ass kid, hahaha.

Next he looked at the big black fishin' line stitches on the top side of my busted foot. I probably had 14 or 15 stitches on each of the two incisions. I know that ain't all that much, and actually my foot ain't that bad compared to those of you who have lost feet or legs in wrecks, or had big steel rods inserted in your bones. I feel for you guys. And I ain't meanin' to whine about my lousy stitches and toe pins, just tellin' what happened, see? So Mister Arrogant Fuckwad looks at the stitches, which I had been playin' with myself the past few days since the soreness and tenderness was lettin' up. Some of them stitches were sorta loose and wiggly while others had kinda grown into the skin and were tight and itchy.

Then he sez "It's time for those stitches to come out." Next he grabbed his little scissors and started snippin' 'em, OK no biggie. Then he pulled out the loose ones which felt kinda good, and then he tugged on the ones that were kinda stuck and that got my attention a little bit, hahaha, but he got all the stitches out. Good, that's progress. And then? He took his three fingers and put each one on the ends of the three stainless steel pins stickin' outta the ends of my toes. And he wiggled them just a little bit. And I nearly flew up to the ceiling, hahaha. OUCH! GAWDAMMIT!

Then he sez "It's time for those pins to come out." And he calls in the nurse and she comes waltzin' in pushin' a stainless steel cart with his Dr. Frankenstein tools on it. They start gabbin' and gettin' busy like they are gonna pull them pins right now. I'm like hey, what's going on here? I looked at the tool cart and noticed there was not a hypodermic needle that would hold a pain shot for me. So I asked the prick, "What about a shot? Is there gonna be some pain involved in this?" And the fuckin' jerk sez "Well,… I'm not going to feel any pain at all." And at first I thought the sumbitch was jokin',… but he ain't.

He had the nurse come over to the side of the table I was a-layin' on and he told her to hold my leg down, so she grabs my leg with both her hands on the top part of my shin up above the cast. Then that so-called doctor fucker took his stainless steel Vise Grip things and clipped it onto the end of the pin on my middle toe. Just the snappin' of the Vise Grips onto the pin sent shivers up my spine. I'm thinkin' to myself, what the fuck is gonna happen next? Then he asked the nurse if she was holdin' my leg down good, she sez yes, and that fucker asshole YANKED them Vise Grips up into the air, maybe a foot or so, and then they slipped off and my foot came crashin' back down to SLAM on the table, and the pain from that made me see stars and my palms sweated. HOLY SHIT! This is worse than the wreck.

Then the asshole calls in another nurse and has her stand on the other side of the table. So now I got one nurse on each side and I'm just thinkin' to myself, hurry the fuck up you fuckin' asshole prick and get this fuckin' shit over with you gawddamn arrogant jerk. Then he had each nurse lay across my leg to hold it down, hahaha! That's right. So now I got four,…yes 4, not a typo…boobs a-layin' on my leg, cuz each one of them nurses had two boobs, see? And two nurse boobs + two nurse boobs = four nurse boobs. How lucky can a horny young chopper guy get, right? Right.

So now the four boobs are layin' on my leg and that asshole clamps the Vise Grips on the pin again, makes me sweat some more, yanks it up, and I felt that fuckin' pin pull out all the way up to the roots of my jaw teeth, and now I knew what REAL PAIN felt like, cuz the Vise Grips slippin' off before were merely a warm up for this depraved torture action. I felt dizzy like I was gonna pass out. Then

I yelled out to the room, "Hurry up and get them other two! Do it now! Get it over with!" So he did. He enjoyed it.

YANK! "OWW, GAWDDAMMIT!" YANK! "OWW, GAWDDAMIT!"

And then it was over, except for all the dark red fresh blood oozin' out the ends of all three toes where the pins had been. The palms of my hands were drippin' sweat. I told Dr. Vasshole, "you are a real jerk for not givin' me a pain shot for that". I hope you have somebody do that to you someday." And he ignored me and left the room like…so what? Fuck you murder-cycle trash boy. I sat in the room for a little while trying to recuperate and not be dizzy. Cuz now I gotta ride the Shovelhead Chopper back home and drown my sorrows in some booze and weed.

On the way outta the office, the gal at the reception desk told me my next appointment would be in 4 more weeks to get the cast off. I said fine, whatever, and hobbled on out. Strapped the crutches back on the girder and rode back home. Got high and drunk.

I never went back to that fucker again. I cut the gawdamn cast off my own damn self. And when I cut it off, it was on a Saturday afternoon when I knew they'd be closed. So, I rode back over to Arlington to their office and I threw the cast parts right in front of their fuckin' front door. Then I rode over to The Solution Club, a fun time beer joint where I used to shoot pool a lot. I could not shoot pool at this busted foot stage, but I sure could drink.

Oh,…and I never paid the fucker his doctor bill. Fuck him and his arrogant shit. I swore to myself that if I EVER saw that fuckin' prick out in public, I was gonna walk up to him and give him just exactly what he deserved, a nice hard core right uppercut to his chin, knocking his ass cold before he ever hit the floor, that's how much I hated,…and still hate,…that fuckin' piece of dog shit. And if that Dr. Vasshole ain't dead today, I hope he is droolin' spit and shittin' his diapers in an old folks' home and I hope his kids hate his guts. And really,…who could blame them?

This picture here is two of those three pins that were in my toes. They were in there sooo far that only about 1/4 inch was sticking out the ends, just enough for the prick to get his Vise Grips on, hahaha.

And I still have the third pin around here somewhere, and it is all sticky, gummy and gooey from resins it got from cleaning bongs. So in its place, I give you one of my favorite and most-used roach clips from the 1970s and you probably had one just like it,…right? I knew it, and there is a dime in there for size reference.

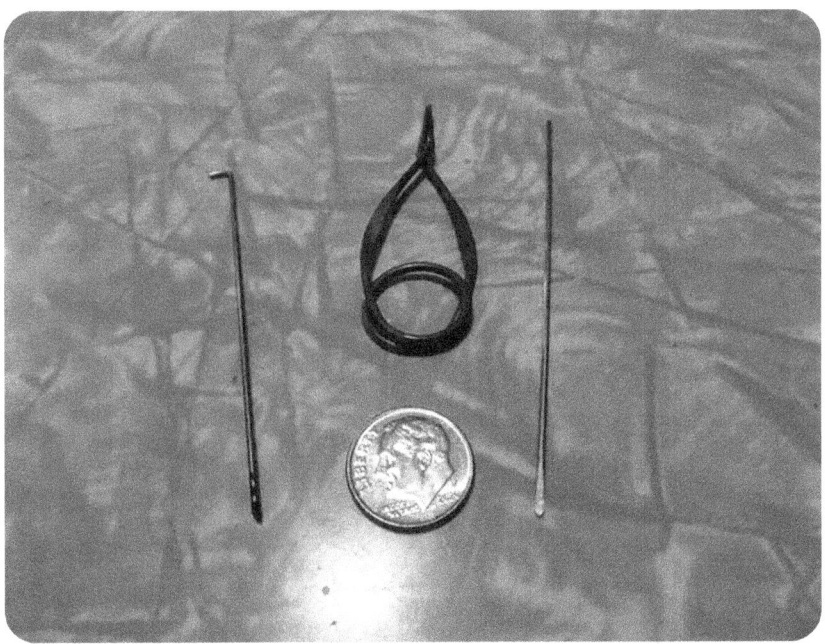

PART 65: "THE EARLY YEARS"

April 1977

Lucky you, here's a picture of my Size 14 foot and 2 of the 3 stainless steel pins that they wired my toes back on, yay! The longest pin is 3 & 1/2 inches long and all 3 of them went right up through the middle of the toe bones to anchor them back on my foot, and they just had 1/4 inch sticking out above the top of the toe nails for the Dr Vasshole to grab with his Vise Grips to yank out.

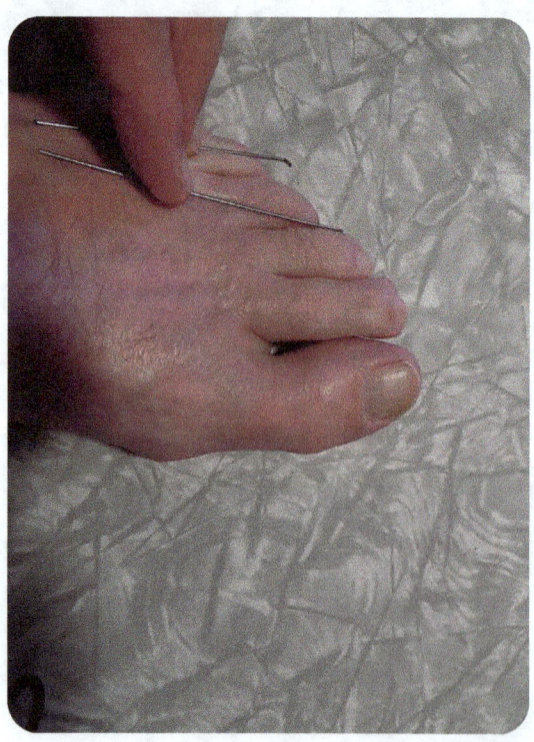

THE EARLY YEARS

Between the lousy docs in Mississippi and the Asshole Dr. Vasshole , this fuckin' foot hurt me all my dang life, especially in the cold winter times. Then a few years ago I finally got lucky when I got cancer,…lymphoma,…and the docs put me on 4 kinds of chemo for 6 months. The chemo killed the nerves in both my feet so now I just have neuropathy. Yay! So I traded in one good foot and one bum foot for two dead feet. I guess that's a wash to kinda break even, eh? And now I gotta take care of the busted girder.

BREAKING NEWS: I just learnt that Doc Vasshole is now daid, pissed off this planet in 2021. I outlived you, you "murder-cycle" fucker. Now the stray dogs can piss on your grave and the worms can eat you, if they don't vomit. A-men.

Part 66: "The Early Years"

Back to Work Ya Bum & Busted Girder Repair May 1977

The busted foot got well enough that I could quit being a dead beat that may or may not have been selling lids for 10 bucks and I could finally go back to work and make a few what they call "honest bucks" for a change. I was also getting ready to graduate carpenter apprentice school in June,…yay! That meant no more riding the chopper at night through freeway traffic over to the other side of Dallas for those night classes. And since the wreck, I had been going to school 4 nights a week to make up for the time I missed when I was in Daytona and the hospital in Mississippi and then in the cast, having all that fun.

So now I'm making around 9 bucks an hour, yippee! That means I was taking home around 300 a week and still had house payments of only 104. That left a lotta free cash for bike stuff. So I could go from being dead broke after the trip to having some moola again. Meanwhile, the +25" over Flame Cut Girder is stil fucked up on the 74 AMF Chopper, and it's being run rigid with the busted shock mount from the crash. I called long distance information… remember them? And after several calls, I eventually found the guy in Southern California who originally made the awesome girder. His name was Bob Olson.

Anyhow, he told me over the phone that he no longer had his shop going. But he did do work outta his garage and yes, he did still have parts for his girders. I told him about the wreck and how the bottom mount for the shock was busted. He told me he could fix it. Yay! So I had the Shovelhead inside the abode, yanked off the girder and made a 3/4 inch plywood crate for it and shipped it off to Southern California on a Greyhound Bus. Bye bye. Bob got it and looked at it, called me back and said sure, he could fix it. So 'The Repair' is gonna happen after all and I'll have a nice girder to run again,...right?

Wrong,...of course. After Bob had the girder a few days, he called me back and told me that he had it welded up good and the new bottom mount for the shock was also good to go. Grand total for the repair was 50 bucks, not too shabby. But first,...since the chrome was fucked up where he just welded it, and since the chrome was kinda fucked up when I got it used at the Dallas swap meet the year before, and since the wreck in Mississippi put a few more dings and scratches on it,...did I wanna have him to get it re-chromed at the chrome shop he used right in his town? He said it would be 125 bucks to get it re-chromed, then it would be perfect like brand new when he shipped it back to me. I said sure, let's go for it. So I sent him a money order for the $125. I called a few days later and he said he got the money order, the girder was now in the chrome shop gettin' shiny and he told me that he told them to do a nice and fast job on it cuz he had to ship it back to Dallas quick.

Then a few days later he called me and said he got it back from the chrome shop and it looked BEAUTIFUL! It was perfect, brand new ready to go again. Great. And he was gonna ship it back to me.

And then? I never heard from Bob again,...groan. And the next time I tried to call him, his phone number had been disconnected. And the girder never showed up. Now,... I ain't sayin' he ripped me off on purpose, but he may have. And then again, maybe something else happened to him and the girder? Maybe his house burned down? Maybe he died? Maybe he got busted and hauled off to jail? Who knows? All I know is,... I was now not only burned for the 175 bucks, I also got burned outta my girder I loved sooo much and I no longer had a front end for the Shovel Chopper. Bummer, dude!

So,...off to the swap meet again in search of a new front end and I'd better find one FAST cuz now it is summer time approaching. I found two lower legs, already shaved, for 40 bucks. And I found a set of triple trees for another 40 bucks, the same triple trees still on the wide glide today, except they've been chromed twice since then, and Shelby helped me out with a set of used wide glide fork tubes which were +15" over, which is what the old Twisted Springer had been, and what the frame was set up best for anyhow. And then I stuck the 5 Spoke Invader mag on it. Presto, Change-O, now I got a new look on the chopper.

Anyhow, I wound up getting this "Emergency Front End" together pretty fast. But the poor sumbitch leaked fork fluid like you wouldn't believe, hahaha. Oh well. At least it was up and running again. And this is the only photo I have of the 74 AMF Chop at this stage and time. And this set up only lasted a little bit, maybe 3 or 4 months, cuz it's getting ready to change again. PS And the squeeze bulb fell off in the wreck the $3.95 Pier 1 Imports Bombay Taxi Horn. I wonder if it is still under warranty?

Part 67: "The Early Years"

Modified Kustom Frame Time

Well, in the summer of 1977 this 22 year old chopper punk took it upon his-self to cut up the 1971 D&D Jammer frame. Yep, gonna chop the chopper frame, hahaha. I liked the sleek look Harold's Panhead Chopper had and I kinda wanted a frame along that idea. And that idea was to hack saw the frame at the front foot pegs area and at the seat area.

Then, over at their custom fabricating shop in Arlington, Dangerous George and Dutch made me a new neck section for this frame. They created a new backbone, new 2 & 1/2 inch longer stretched down tubes with a kool slight kick at the top, and what I really liked best, a new neck itself, both slim-line and streamline lookin', no more of those garden variety common everyday bulges at the top and bottom of the neck bearing areas.

And no more double gussets on the outsides of the frame neck. It's been converted into one simple clean gusset on the inside center of the frame neck, oooh la la, hahaha. This new creation frame is now gonna make my chopper look a little bit different from the rest. The neck is gonna sit up higher and the motor is gonna sit a little bit lower, giving a lower center of gravity which = better handling. Not too shabby thinkin' for a 22 year old's mind, eh?

And here I am with the newly finished frame creation in the back of my dad's White Chevy Pick-Em-Up. Now all I gotta do is build up another chopper,…right? Right. And I did all of this in less than a month. Imagine that time frame today? I can't. But I kinda cheated, cuz I did not need a new motor and tranny build just yet, so I set them aside in the living room where we always had the Smoke &

SHOVELHEAD DAVE

Juice Sessions. And I did not mold this frame, either, or have it professionally sprayed. It is still good ol' dependable Rattle Can Black, and check out them Holy Jeans! Holy shit.

PART 68: "THE EARLY YEARS"

The New Look for Summer 1977

And this is what I came up with for the summer of 1977. It's the 74 AMF Chopper's 4th different look so far since September 1975. And what we got here is the new custom built frame from Dangerous George and Dutch, Shelby's 84 inch motor build with the Jerry Branch 44 mm Mikuni, the fully Andrews equipped tranny that Harold built, and open Phase 3 belt drive with Barnett clutch. It still has the hand clutch and foot shift at this point, but not for much longer.

I cut off the back fender and got rid of the sissy bar, flipped the tail light upside down. Stuck on a Bates solo seat and P-Pad that I found at another swap meet. Them original old Bates seats are worth their weight in gold today. I made those exhaust pipes myself outta two sets. The fronts were just regular drag pipes and the back halves were regular muffler pipes. What I did was kinda sneaky, but it worked.

Before I welded the two sections together, I took out the baffles in the muffler parts… Then I ran a nice hidden rust proof stainless steel sheet metal screw in from the motor side of the pipes into the center of the pipe, about half way up in there. Then I welded the rest together and put 'em on the chopper. So what that did was give it straight pipes but they looked like they had mufflers. And if a cop thought it was too fuckin' loud and tried to run his billy club up in there to check, his club would hit the sheet metal screw so he'd think it had baffles. See there? Kinda sneaky shit for a 22 year old punk chopper builder, huh? And them pipes sounded really good, too. They had a nice deep rumble to them, thanks especially to the stroker motor.

Only problem with the pipes was,…if ya look at the bottom of the front pipe, it is kinda mashed flat, cuz it would scrape when I went around corners kinda tight and fast, hahaha. As for the front end? Still the old leaky swap meet wide glide with the Invader 5 Spoke. And that head light is the same one that came off the +15" over Twisted Springer. Those front foot pegs are the old #1 pegs I still run today. Got my money's worth outta them suckers, huh?

Part 69: "The Early Years"

Summer-Fall 1977

Here's two other shots of the 74 AMF Chopper, one with the old cowboy leather saddle bags. And yes, I still have those saddle bags, out there hangin' on the garage wall right next to my old spurs and bull rope from 1971 when I rode bulls, hahaha.

And my oh my, look who's back? My buddy Freddie, the guy that I sold the old Red 67 Sportster to, got married and his wife made him stop riding them dangerous motorsickles, she made him sell it back to me, thank ya kindly Donna ma'am. And I even got it back for 500 bucks cheaper than I sold it to him for, cuz he let it fall to shit and it wasn't running. And I sold it to him in the spring of 1974, so he let it go to shit in just 3 years? Oh well.

I tuned the Sportster up and got it running good again. Put in fresh engine and tranny oils, new battery, adjusted the brakes, and it was good to go. Only one problem? It didn't fit me. I was 6 foot 4 now and that nice Sportster was too cramped for me. So I sold it to another high school buddy named Alan around Christmas time, 1977.

SHOVELHEAD DAVE

Part 70: "The Early Years"

Fall 1977

As if 1977 wasn't a busy enough of a year for me back in Dallas, from the Daytona trip with 3 break downs, to the busted foot, to the +25" over flame cut girder gettin' ripped off,… I mean,…umm "gone",…to the Shovelhead's fast tear down and then the chopper frame getting cut up for the new neck section and then the newest build on the 74 AMF Chopper with the Bates solo seat,…well…then we somehow found time to put Brudder Charles' 71 Shovelhead into a Paughco frame he got from Shelby's shop, Mid Cities Choppers. Ain't we the busy little fuckers,… I mean,…beavers?

And that Durfee girder on Charles' 71 Shovel chopper is the one he got from Stan, the very same Durfee that rope towed me to Valdosta Georgia and the very same Durfee I run on the 74 AMF today. How's that for "what goes around comes around"? I now run the very same Durfee what-done rope towed me back in 1977 behind Stan's Pan/Shovel chopper. That Mach 1 was Charles' and it had the 351 Cleveland in it with the 4 Speed and Shaker Hood.

Part 71: "The Early Years"

So 1978 Rolls Around in Dallas

And here's where I sold out and went all Fancy Hoidy Toidy on everyone, bwahaha. Since my first chop build in September 1975 with the Twisted Springer, everything on the 74 AMF had always been built with old used parts that came from Dallas and Fort Worth swap meets or else they came outta Shelby's old used parts bin, see? It had been a true Swap Meet Special up until right now.

So here's the brand new Rudy-Poo Candy-Ass version with,… wait for it now,…a brand fuckin' new front end to go with that recently modified frame from Dangerous George and Dutch. Bahahaha, that's right, I finally bought something new for the chopper that nobody else had ever fucked before,… I mean, fucked with before. This is a brand spankin' new cherry virgin front end. But what is it? What is that strange creature not too many folks are familiar with? Is it a totally rigid fork tube front end? Nope. Did it come from outer space? Nope.

THE EARLY YEARS

It's a +15" over brand new fork, with new tubes from Frank's Forking and them wild Barney Sliders down there on the bottom. And those Barneys were the new hot thing back then and they got away with being really slim lookin' cuz they had teflon bushings in them.

To go with the new front fork is a brand new 21 inch front wheel (which I still have) that I got at Brown's Custom Cycles in Dallas on Main Street and that rim was like an outrageous $19.95 back then. And on that new rim is a new Avon tire, of course. Still no front brake. And there's the brand new Drag Specialties Butt Buckets front seat that I got at the swap meet in Dallas for 20 bucks. Yes, it came from a swap meet, sure, but it ain't used, it's brand new and was still in the plastic bag when I got it which means nobody ever sat and farted on it,...yet. Also we got some brand new one piece drag handlebars to replace the old drag bars which had the old swap meet risers. And there's a brand fuckin' new head light added to the mix.

And lookie what else is new on there now? Notice there ain't no more clutch lever on the handlebars? Yep, this is my first build with the suicide clutch and slap stick. The tranny still has the ratchet lid on top, so it is not a pure jockey shift with positions, instead you slap it back and forth to change gears. Had I ever ridden one before? Of course not. I just built the bike up with it on there and went for it. Was it kinda scary at first? Of course it was, hahaha. That's the fun of choppers, building up some dangerous loud shit that scares people. I just hopped on it the day I finished it and took off with the suicide clutch, stick shift and no front brake. Why not? And there is a brand new kick stand on this side, too, longer than the stock one.

    I might shoulda cut some links outta that chain to pull the back wheel a bit more forward, cuz that is a big gap from the front of the back tire to the fender in my opinion today, but what the fuck? I was 23 now and just having fun.

    And speaking of turnin' 23, that also means I was now a full-fledged journeyman carpenter and made almost 10 whole bucks an hour at this time. And the things on the other side of this chopper build sorta became my trademark and stood out for the next 8 years until the 1988 tear down in Seattle. But you'll hafta wait to see a carb side photo to see what it is. I still can't get over it. Makin' almost 10 bucks an hour, wow! No wonder I could afford all them new chopper parts, "We're rich, Wyatt." -Billy.

Part 72: "The Early Years"

Dallas, January 1978

Here we have the semi-excitin' carb side of the most recent version of the 74 AMF Chopper. That's my sweet little niece Donna on there and she's holding my new pup Rosco. Rosco used to go Chopper Ridin' with me. I'd carry him inside my jacket with his head stickin' out in front, hahaha. He loved the wind. He was a cool,…cool,…puppy.

Donna's over 50 today and I don't know where Rosco is. Have you seen him? He liked to dig holes under the fence and run away sometimes. He liked to eat a lot. Plus he loved to chase cats and bicycles and he'd bite mean people that deserved it.

SHOVELHEAD DAVE

Oh, and there's the new-fangled hoidy toidy fancy upsweep fishtail pipes, yikes! Damn, did them fuckers sound good. And one very important thing about runnin' fishtails is this,…the fuckin' cops can't get their billy clubs up in there, maybe their peckers might fit in there, but not the billy clubs. If they asked if I had mufflers in there, I'd just say,…of course.

Part 73: "The Early Years"

Spring 1978 Road Trip

OK,… OK,…so much for all this hangin' around the house and workin' out in the garage shit, drinkin' suds, turnin' wrenches, smokin' weed and listenin' to 1970s kick ass rock & roll cranked up loud wastin' all that gawdamn time buildin' up them two loud fancy Shovelhead choppers. Iz us guys gonna hit the road on 'em or iz we just gonna hang around lookin' at the choppers all the damn time tryin' to impress the citizen neighbors? In other words, what I'm gettin' at is,…do them two Shovelhead choppers actually run or are they just for show and tell, or shits and giggles for the Sidewalk Commandos to admire and drool over?

Well, gee whiz, gimme a fuckin' break, we've been kinda busy buildin' them two choppers, ya know? So ya don't gotta get yer panties in a bind and get so riled up. OK, fuck a duck, let's hit the road again already, sheesh. This time it's gonna be Baby Brudder Charles on his now finely chopped 71 Shovelhead with Stan's old Durfee Girder,…the same girder that Stan rope- towed me with in Georgia in 1977, and I'll be on the new Barney Sliders version of the ol' 74 AMF Chopper.

Let's hit the road. We're headed up to Oklahoma first to visit Cuzzin Johnny and our kin folks for a little bit, and then we're gonna head east across eastern Oklahoma and get headed on up by Cherokee Nation and then into the north of Arkansas in the Ozarks to set up camp somewhere's around Fayetteville. And then from there, we'll ride up into southern Missouri Ozarks to their Bull Shoals Lake area. Fayetteville will be our main campin' hangout and we're gonna do

SHOVELHEAD DAVE

some day trips around that area in the Ozark Mountains. We've each got one week off work to do it. Sounds like a fun ride, huh?

Let's kick them two Shovelheads over and hit the road.

What? Kick 'em BOTH over? Wait a dang minnit. Back in the 1975 Road Trip, Charles' 71 Shovel was an FL with electric start only. Now it has kick start? Yep, it sure does. And you were very smart to pick up on that, cuz you've been payin' very close attention to this crap,…right? I knew it, hahaha. Here we are out on the road in what they call the Tall Pine Country.

Part 74: "The Early Years"

Spring 1978 Road Trip in Arkansas

We woke up in our pup tents the next day, kicked over and rode the two Shovel Choppers up by Eureka Springs in the Ozarks. When we were little kids in the 1960s, our folks used to drive us up to Eureka Springs in their old 1950 Mercury, the 4 door type with the suicide doors on back and the big sun visor on top of the windshield. We'd sit in the back seat and hang onto that rope-cord thing that ran across the back of the front seat. Probably drove our folks nuts.

We'd also collect nice smooth little rocks along the way and keep 'em in the back seat's floorboard, cuz we had us two sling shots and we'd shoot rocks at the road signs as we drove along. It was free entertainment. The metal signs would pop nice and loud when we occasionally hit one, hahaha. Those are some great memories.

Our folks used to get a room at The Joy Motel on the edge of town there cuz it had a fun swimmin' pool with a big high diving board, which they don't allow anymore cuz everybody has to sue everybody when their dumb kids do dumb shit and get hurt,…right? Right. Anyhow, there was also an ice cream joint nearby that gave nice big single dip cones for 7 cents a dip. Wish I could step into a Time Machine and go back to them days for a bit,…or maybe forever.

And here's one special thing I remember about this ride this second day that I will never forget.

We left kinda early in the morning, headed for Eureka Springs, and on the way there, when we got up kinda high in the Ozarks, there was a big Look Out Tower up on top of the hill on the left side of the road, like maybe an old forest rangers' fire lookout that had been converted into a tourist trap?

SHOVELHEAD DAVE

It was like a little cabin up on stilts. You'd pay 50 cents or whatever it was and then got the 'fun time' of climbin' a whooooole bunch of stairs to get up really high. And once you got up there on top, you could see for miles and miles, lookin' over the trees out to the tops of the Ozarks in the distance. Well, that ain't got nuthin' to do with this part of the story anyhow, wink, wink.

What I was gettin' at was acrost the street from the Look Out Tower. A Mom & Pop cafe with THE best Ham Steak Breakfast I ever et in all my lives. And when I say a ham steak, I don't mean a cheap ass piece of fake ham shit they give you today at I-Hop or Denny's or Lenny's. It was a slab of fresh ham, maybe a half inch thick, that was grilled with the bone still in it and we got that and 3 eggs and some taters that were not frozen hash browns, but were sliced like silver dollars (remember them?) and they put them on your overflowin' plate, too. It was some of the best breakfast eats I ever had.

And here it is now, 2022 and I still remember their nice place and their awesome food on the side of the road out kinda in the middle of nowhere up in the Ozarks. If any of your folks are from there or have traveled there, maybe you know the place where we went.

And I ain't admittin' to doin' nuthin' illegal here. For all anybody knows, I may or may not have been smokin' some corn husks, or grapevine, or candy cigarettes, or banana peels, or jerky, or frog legs. All I know is it's very relaxin' to unwind after a nice day's ride, that's all. And don't anybody run off with my Dingo Boots, hahaha. I got my eye on you,…the good one.

PART 75: "THE EARLY YEARS"

Spring 1978 Road Trip in Arkansas

We wuz ridin' along in Arkansas this fine morning on them two Dallas Shovelhead Choppers and came upon this loud ass thing, don't really know what it was. But it was hissin' that steam out and there was a loud bell ringin' so I took this picture of it when we rode by on the Shovelheads.

I guess it don't do much for ya if ya can't hear the damn things going off. Bummer. But it reminded me of that scene in Easy Rider where Wyatt and Billy were ridin' their choppers by all that loud work shit that was going on in the background. So this is our cheapie version of it. Yu'll hafta use your imagination, wink, wink.

PART 76: "THE EARLY YEARS"

Spring 1978 Road Trip in Arkansas

The next day we rode up into Missouri to the Bull Shoal Lake area. Nice country to ride through, for sure. We even did some tourist shit. We took a dang boat ride, fer cryin' out loud, hahaha. Us? Two Texas chopper guys? On a boat out in the Missouri lake? Oh well. The boat had a nice purdy little gal drivin' it around, and ain't boat steerin' wheels supposed to be on the right hand side? This one's on the left like a car. Oh well. Hope it don't sink. And I hope both the choppers are still there when we get done with this boat trip.

THE EARLY YEARS

And this-here other picture ain't no Arkansas Razorback and it ain't no Ozark Bigfoot. It's my little 21 year old baby brudder, all 6 foot 4 or 5 and 225 pounds of him. He was a good back up guy, or body guard for me, hahaha. I was really nice to him at this stage in our lives so's he didn't get pissed off at me and pick me up and throw me somewheres like up in a big tall tree where I couldn't get back down.

And the next photo is some other thing that was going on out in the middle of the Ozark Mountains. Riding through this area was kinda funny. Cuz with the Ozarks and tall trees everywhere, you might tend to think you are waaaay out in the woods somewhere with nobody around for miles and miles. But then ya ride around a big loopy bend in the road and run into stuff like this out there. Maybe this was a paper factory? I dunno.

PART 77: "THE EARLY YEARS"

Spring 1978 Road Trip in Arkansas

Here's another shot of our two Shovelhead Choppers resting in the shade. The camping had been fun and the food had been fantastic. One thing them Ozark folks know how to do is eat, and we had some of the best bar-be-que ever. Whether we got brisket or ribs or chicken or hot links, it was tasty stuff. And good sides like tater salad, fried okra, and baked beans with the little chunks of sausage in it. Hell, that coulda been Jimmy Dean Sausage in them beans for all we know, hahaha, and that's top shelf stuff right there. And cold frosty beer to wash it all down with is always nice.

I've found few things in life as much fun as gettin' an early morning buzz going, having a nice big breakfast and then heading outside to kick over Shovelheads and take off riding through some mountains. Ride a coupla hours, stop to get gas and stretch your legs and do another puff or two when there ain't nobody lookin'.

Then kick them choppers over and take off with an even better buzz. Just riding through the woods, up and down the hills, around the twisty corners, into the shade then back into the sun, smelling the different smells in the woods that the folks in cars are totally unaware of and never get to experience. And let's face it,…some things in life just plain stink. Like maybe that recently road kilt skunk we just rode by,… PEEEEE-YOOOOO! But even that is funny, hahaha. Just don't hit it and get that shit on your wheels. And as these last vacation road trip days ticked by, we knew we'd be leaving the beautiful Ozarks soon and be headed back to city traffic and our jobbie-jobs. So we enjoyed it while we could.

PART 78: "THE EARLY YEARS"

Spring 1978 Road Trip in Arkansas

Didya ever go ridin' and campin' with somebody who took sneaky photos of you and you had no idea they did it until you got back home and got the film developed and then there it was, bwa-haha? I ain't exactly lookin' for Arkansas Razorbacks in the woods.

And here's the nice big tall tree area where we were camped. I do not remember it being a KOA Kampground cuz it was more of a rustic place. (That's a high-falutin' way of sayin' that's why I'm peein' in the woods.) And the last photo looks like some more puffin' is going on. This fun road trip is nearly over,…sniff.

THE EARLY YEARS

PART 79: "THE EARLY YEARS"

Spring 1978 Road Trip in Arkansas

Brudder Charles risked his life and took this picture whilst we were flyin' down the Arkansas highway. This road trip is coming to an end now. And it had a really strange ending. What was the strange ending?

Nuthin' happened! That's right. When it was over, we just rode back home to Dallas on the Shovel choppers, unpacked the road gear and each of us went inside our houses and got ready for work the next day. Ain't that pretty fuckin' weird?

Compare this Arkansas Road Trip to the 1973 Canada Road Trip where Cuzzin Paul and me got separated and lost each other up at the Canadian Border and there weren't no cell phones back then so each of us had to ride home alone. Or compare this trip to the 1975 Road Trip where Cuzzin Johnny joined Charles and me for the swing through the western states and then lost all our money in Las Vegas and had to ride home with no money for food, just making it on gas fumes and pennies, hahaha.

Or compare it to the 1977 Daytona Trip where I didn't even get to ride home cuz of the crash in Mississippi and ended up in the hospital. So this trip had a nice boring normal end to it. Yay! It was a successful Chopper Road Trip,…no tickets, no going broke, no getting separated, no wrecks, no broken bones. And it was a successful road trip with my very own Baby Brudder so it made it all that much more fun.

THE EARLY YEARS

    Now,…as for that cheapie cute little helmet on back? Geeze, hahaha. It's got its own story. Just before Texas got rid of their helmet law, I was ridin' with a black Arthur Fuller helmet that had a chrome ring around the edge, ooh la la, fancy shit, lemme tell ya. And on one trip where I rode to Oklahoma and back, I got caught up in one of those Texas Monsoon Storms out by Denton and the helmet got totally soaked inside,…just like I was totally soaked on the outside. So I had that helmet sittin' out on my porch drying off.

    And then the next day,…it was gone. I don't know if some kid got it or maybe a dog carried it off to chew on? All I know is, it was gone. And there was only like 2 weeks to go until the helmet law was gonna be gone. But, I still needed a helmet for those two weeks.

    So early one Saturday morning I rode the Shovel chop without a helmet over to the Army & Navy Surplus store in Arlington to get this very helmet in this photo, cuz it was only like 5 or 7 bucks or so, compared to 40 or 50 bucks for a real helmet. And then when I got about 7 or 8 blocks from the Army store, I got pulled over by a cop and got a ticket. And then the fucker made me leave the chopper on the side of the street in a parking spot where I had to put money in the meter and then I had to WALK to the fuckin' Army store to get this helmet. And yes, I still have it out in the garage.

PART 80: "THE EARLY YEARS"

End of the 1978 Arkansas Road Trip

This photo right here is the very last photo of these two Shovelhead Choppers together. Sigh.

After our Arkansas Road Trip was over in the spring of 1978, Brudder Charles was out riding his 71 Shovel Chopper with our old Panhead ridin' buddy Slick, from the 1977 Daytona story.

They were ridin' along down Carrier Parkway over in Grand Prairie Texas, doin' maybe 40 or so, according to Charles. Two lanes going north, two lanes going south, divided concrete median strip in the middle. An intersection came up and Charles and Slick had the green light and rode on through just like normal, only to have this pimple faced little kid jerk in his daddy's car run right through the red light, which T-Boned Charles.

Since he was knocked clear of his Shovelhead, Charles went rolling and rolling and sliding down the concrete street. No broken bones but tons of road rash. Meanwhile, the kid's car knocked the 71 Shovel Chopper in half. That's right. The kid snapped the fork stem outta the Durfee girder. The girder and front wheel went one way, the rest of the chopper went the other way. When all the scrapin' and slidin' was over and the dust settled, Slick came up to Charles to see if he was OK. (Now I wasn't there, but both of them told me identical versions of this story right after it happened, so that is my source.)

When Slick saw that Charles was semi-OK, he suddenly went livid, totally outta control, hahaha. Slick started in yelling and screamin' at the snot nosed kid. Then Slick pointed to the gas station over on the corner and yelled out to the kid "You run your fuckin' ass over to that gas station and call the fuckin' cops right now!"

With all the weed Slick usually had on him that was a rather strange request, but that's what happened, hah. So then Charles said the kid looked down at the ground like he was being grounded or something and started walking off to the gas station. This drove Slick even madder and crazier. Charles, who was still sittin' on the ground, said Slick ran up behind the kid and yells out "I SAID RUN MOTHERFUCKER!"…and then hauled off with his steel toed boot and kicked the kid in the butt like he was the Dallas Cowboys Field Goal kicker who was kicking a 70 yard field goal, Charles said when Slick kicked him in the ass, he saw both the kid's feet go up in the air, Slick kicked him in the ass soooo hard.

So then the kid gets the message and started running to the gas station. And while the kid was gone, Enraged Slick blew up even more and started kicking in the car. Charles said he started up front left where the kid had hit him, and Slick kicked in the left front quarter panel, then kicked in the driver's door, then the rear left quarter panel, then went over to the other side and kicked in the door and both quarter panels on the passenger side. He left the bumpers alone, cuz they were probably harder steel, hah. So that was what happened in the wreck.

After all the carnage had settled and the cops left and all that shit, Slick rode back to his house, parked his Panhead, jumped in his Good Times Van and drove back to the scene and they loaded up Charles' chopper, which was now in two pieces. And now it gets even worse. For a few weeks the two pieces of the chopper sat in his back yard under the big oak tree. The Durfee and front wheel on one side, the chassis,…frame motor tranny back wheel,…on the other side. And then?

Even though it was in his back yard, and even though there was a fence, and even though he had a funny & trusty loud mouthed Beagle named Bullet who howled so loud you could hear him 2 blocks away,…somehow,…some low life scum bag thieves removed the boards from the fence and got in there and stole the back half of his chopper.

They apparently saw the Durfee was busted, so they left that there on the ground. Then they put the fence boards back in place to make it look kinda normal. Charles never found his 71 Shovelhead. And he was sooo disgusted at this point that he never got another bike. He gave me the busted Durfee, and that's what I hauled around all these years until I finally got it fixed in 2020 by a guy in Michigan named Sprocket that I found on Facebook, of all things. And that Durfee is the old one that Stan rope towed me with and it was Charles' old Durfee and now it's on the 74 AMF Chopper out in the garage.

Part 81: "The Early Years"

July 18, 1978,… Holy Shit

After the Brudder Charles Arkansas/Missouri Road Trip, I decided I needed two things back on the 74 AMF Chopper. And they both hafta do with haulin',…can ya guess what they are?

If you guessed a back seat and bigger sissy bar, you got it correct. And ya might find this kinda hard to believe,… I know I did,…but at a swap meet over yonder in Fort Worth, lookie what I found! I got the matching Drag Specialties Butt Bucket seat for the back end for 20 bucks, just what I paid for the front one. Now how is that even possible? And they both got the red crushed velvet diamond seat inserts, what are the chances of that shit even happening? I got the front seat months earlier over in Dallas, just by itself, no other seats around, it was still in the brand new plastic bag, and then to find its mate about 30 miles away over in Fort Worth several months later? And this back seat was also still in its plastic bag, never been used. I nearly wet my Levis, the Chopper Gods musta been with me that day.

And other finds at this swap meet were that big ass Pregnant Guppy lookin' gas tank, the new 6-inch flat rear fender, and the sissy bar. The sissy bar was a good size and I just put it in the vise and bent it a little bit to make the angles fit to the seat and new fender. And that gas tank was a special find, and I got no idea who made it. It was a little bit big for my personal tastes on a chopper, but it had a really cool feature that made me overlook its mammoth size. It had one of those Pop-Up Gas Caps, the kind that is hidden and fits flush to the tank. There was a spine going through the center of the tank, and you'd twist the spine and the hidden cap would pop up for gas.

SHOVELHEAD DAVE

Now of course, finding all this swap meet treasure meant one thing and one thing only. Pull the 74 AMF Chopper apart and re-do it again, hahaha. OK, no biggie, cuz by this time I was gettin' really good and fast at it. I could have the chopper pulled down to a bare frame inside the house with just hand tools in 5 hours and sometimes less. See there? That's how havin' belt drive open primaries helps you out when it's time to turn the wrenches.

So I brought the chopper into the house again, dropped the needle on the record on the turntable, got out the cold frosty beer, lit up the big fattie, and went in to work doing this version. I had to tear it all down cuz I had to mount the new rear fender, which was also the good ol' Rattle Can Black, got it mated up to the back of the horseshoe oil tank, mounted the back seat from the bottom side of the new back fender, ran new wiring for the tail light and running light, got the license tag situated and put it all back together. I just set the front end over in the corner cuz I didn't hafta do anything to that at this time. No sweat, eh? And then something else happened this July. Gulp.

As if all that work wasn't enough, I decided I needed to pick up this 1969 Corvette. Ain't it purdy? Looks like it's got a few scratches on it though. Hmm. Oh well, it's still a Red big block 427 with 4 speed, black top and interior. Nice, eh? Price was $1,350. What a good deal, huh? It was delivered to my house on the back of a hook, as in, a tow truck. When the tow truck driver was dropping it off on the street in front of the house, he started to leave. I'm like "Hey! Wait a minnit! I need help gettin' this thing into my drive way." I offered him 5 bucks and a cold frosty Lone Star if he'd help push it, and he did.

So now I got another headache,... I mean "fun project" to work on. Plus I still had that ratty primered 63 Sting Ray that was the ex-drag race car, anyhow I got the 69 running in a few days. New battery, oil and fluids, plugs, points and condenser, fired right up. And since I knew a guy that worked at a local trim shop, I got a new black soft top for it and new black carpet. The seats were still good to go, no rips or tears. And the radio even worked, yay!

And a few weeks later when I was trying to start in on the fiberglass body work on it, a guy saw it in the driveway and offered me some money for it, 2,500 clams, so it went on down the road. I wonder if it is still out there somewhere? Maybe the current owner thinks he has an original low mileage cream puff Corvette,...could be the story the snake-oil used car salesman told him?

Part 82: "The Early Years"

Fall 1978

Well,...shit,...that previous version of the 74 AMF Chopper from the summer didn't last very long at all, less than 2 months, maybe even less than 1 month, hahaha, yikes! What happened to it? Mainly was them Barney Sliders. They looked a lot cooler than they worked. They were good for a show bike, they were good for puttin' around town and good for hittin' the bars. Sittin' in a bar's parking lot at night they looked really cool with the street lights makin' their chrome glow really nice. But that Arkansas Road Trip showed me they weren't really up to handlin' heavy duty road use. For heavy duty road use, I needed a heavy duty front end, so back to the swap meets again.

At the Dallas swap, I found these two virgin cherry lower legs, still had all the tabs on 'em, too. 40 bucks. I got that chrome front fender over at Brown's Custom Cycle on Main Street in downtown Dallas, $19.95 it was. (Still have it today, but it's since been painted black and now silver blue.) And no front brake, still suicide clutch and stick shift. And what happens next after I got the lower legs bead blasted and the nice front end all put together and back on the chopper? A crash, of course.

One fine afternoon I was ridin' along on Highway 360 in Arlington, headed north towards DFW Airport. The ride had started out fine, anyhow, but then a slight drizzly rain came in. Oh well, no biggie. I've been wet before, right? It was around 4 or 5 in the afternoon, moderate heavy traffic. I'm in the far left side lane, cars behind me, cars over to the side in the other lanes to the right side.

THE EARLY YEARS

There was a big grass median between the north bound and south bound lanes. Like maybe 50 feet of grass, dipping down in the center like it had been a drainage ditch before? And I'm riding along minding my own bid-ness when suddenly, in the light rain, I spy a big ol' yeller Plymouth Fury up ahead and it is sitting in the grass median,…like what the fuck? It looked like it was sittin' at a fuckin' red light getting ready to cross an intersection that wasn't there. Did it spin out? Is it broken down? I let off on the throttle some to see what the car was doing. Hmm. Nothing, really, just sittin' there like maybe it was outta gas? I got no idea.

Then, at the last second, that fuckin' Plymouth came pulling up onto the road, IN MY LANE, and then? It just stopped. That's right. I now have a parked car sittin' right in my lane, while I'm doing 55 or so, and have cars all around me. Like what the hell am I supposed to do now? I got ready to hit the back mechanical brake, but it was too late. The fucker driving that car looked me right in the eye. We had eye to eye contact, so I KNEW he saw me coming. And then? He pulled out some more, maybe five more feet into the highway and then just panicked and stopped again. I knew I was a goner at this stage. I could almost feel the impact of the car, hear the metal crunchin' and saw myself flyin' over its hood out to the highway. But somehow at the last milli-second, the bike veered to the right, around to the front of the car,…in the slippery road rain.

I missed him,…almost. The 74 AMF Chopper skimmed right by that fucker's right side front bumper doing 55 or so. My left foot,…yes, THAT left foot that just got outta the cast a few months before,…hit the idiot's front bumper. And when my left foot hit his bumper, it shot my left knee up by my head. And my sore left foot then shot backward and my boot heel caved in the oil tank. The impact knocked off the clutch pedal and caved in the shifter handle. The chopper veered violently to the right from the impact, and wobbled and nearly went down,…at 55 mph or so. And the cars behind me woulda run my ass over but good. I coulda been hamburger meat.

But I managed to keep control of the machine, waved my arms like a maniac to the traffic behind me, and pulled it over onto the right side shoulder of the highway, where I sat and just shook with anger and rage and fear, all combined. Immediately, a Toyota pick up pulling a flat bed trailer pulled right up behind me, and two Mexican guys got out and asked if I was OK. They said they saw the entire incident. And then the Yellow Plymouth Fury Asshole came pulling in and he got out of his car. The first thing I noticed was he smelled like booze.

The staggerin' drunk asked me if I was OK. I said "I'm still alive, no thanks to you, you fuckin' asshole!" Then we started discussin' the incident while the other two guys stood there. Then the drunkard started preaching to me, saying how dangerous bikes were and how lucky I am to still be alive. I told him "The main problem bikes have on the road is drunk fuckers like YOU in cars hitting us!"

Meanwhile the two Toyota guys asked if I wanted them to go call the cops. I said yes. Then the drunk gets all scared, begs me not to do that.

I said "I want the cops here so they can see what you did to my chopper." He asked me how much damage did I think it was? I told him probably 500 bucks. (It was stuff I coulda fixed for under 100 bucks, but I was being dramatic right then, and rightfully so.) And then next, that drunk asshole starts saying how he is an American Airlines pilot and was on his way to DFW Airport. He didn't have time to get the cops involved, cuz he had a plane to catch! A drunk pilot flying an American Airlines plane? How nice. And then that drunk fucker yanked out his wallet and he peeled off 5 hunnerd dollar bills and asked me if that was OK with me. I said yeah, I guess so. And then the drunk jumped in his Plymouth Fury and took off,... even headed in the right direction this time,...to go fly the plane fulla innocent passengers and then the two Toyota guys split.

So that left me standing there on the side of the road in the rain with a busted clutch pedal. Now if ya wanna have some fun suicide clutch experience sometime, try ridin' one with a busted clutch pedal in the rain about 18 miles back home without stopping. Just keep jammin' that stick shift back and forth with no clutch, hahaha. It's a real gas, lemme tell ya. Meanwhile, in this photo, you can still see where the rubber bumper peeled off onto the left lower leg. See that black rubber on there? That is Plymouth Fury rubber, hah. At this

THE EARLY YEARS

stage of events, I had already put on a new clutch pedal, of course, but you can still see where my left heel caved in the oil tank. And that means now I gotta tear the 74 AMF Chopper all down again to put in a new oil tank. Ain't this gettin' semi-interestin' now?

And in this view, you can see how that spine hidden gas cap fits flush on the tank.

Part 83: "The Early Years"

More From Fall 1978

Here's one more shot of what the drunk American Airlines pilot did to the 74 AMF Chopper's nice original Harley oil tank,… that fucker. And this is a good view of what the Drag Specialties Butt Buckets looked like. And yes, I still run those same seat pans today, although I have heavily modified them. If ya ride with a center fill horseshoe oil tank, these seats are THE set up. All ya gotta do is tilt the front seat forward and you got easy access to the oil fill and battery. When you are out on road trips checking oil alla time, this pays off. Keepin' it simple. Who wants to waste time unbolting' and re-boltin' seats off and on just to check oil and the battery?

Answer: Not me.

THE EARLY YEARS

And meanwhile, on the Corvette Home Front, I got this puppy for $4,250. Beautiful blue 427 with 4 Speed, blue interior white rag top. It lasted only a few months. Best friend got married, the night of his bachelor party at the stripper joint, Brudder Charles and me totalled it, wiped out doin' over 100 mph racing another Corvette. Blew him away with his 350 auto.

I lost control on the high rise bridges in downtown Dallas. We were up on the top deck, hit the joint in the road doing maybe 130 or so, however fast one of these fuckers goes with the pedal pushed all the way down to the floor for 1 or 2 minutes. The Vette got light in the front, like it was on ice. I over corrected and hit the guard rail on the top bridge. I thought we were gonna go through the guard rail and plummet down to our deaths. I thought I'd done kilt my Baby Brudder and me, and was wonderin' how pissed off our folks were gonna get when they found out I kilt us.

But instead? Big chunks of fiberglass just broke off. Nothing' happened to us, it was like sitting in your couch at home. We just slid and spun and slid and spun like we were on ice. When we slowed down to maybe 60 or 70 mph, I got control and we were even headed in the right direction. Yay! I pulled off the freeway down to the Dupont Plaza and we got outta the car and looked at it. Holy shit. It was,…umm,…gone. That's right, hahaha. The entire front end of the car was gone, just the radiator hangin' out, hissin' and steamin', and the right front quarter was gone, the passenger door skin was gone and you could see the window through it, the right rear quarter was gone, the entire back end was gone, just the spare tire tub and gas tank hanging out, and the left rear quarter was gone.

BUT! I still had the driver's door on there, yay! So now we're drivin' back to my house on the old Highway 80, goin' slow with no lights and the front end is wobblin' cuz the front wheels are knocked outta whack. And then? Here comes those flashin' red lights, hahaha. And the Dallas cop pulled us over and asked what the hell happened to us? I told him we just had a wreck. He asked if anybody else was involved. I said no. The cop pulls out his ticket book. And then Brudder Charles said one of the smartest and luckiest things he ever said in his entire life.

Charles said: "I see you just got your brand-new squad car. Our older brother just got his, too." The cop looked up at us and asks, "You boys got a brother on the police department?" Charles said "Yeah, Danny P, you know him?" Cop said yeah. Then he sez, "Look, since you guys are OK and nobody else was involved, I'm lettin' you go. Just pretend you never saw me here tonight and let me get outta here first." We said OK and he drove away. I made it the rest of the way home doing 25 or 30 mph and the poor 68 Big Block Vette was totalled. One drag race guy bought the motor, tranny and rear end, another guy got the interior, so it got parted out.

Part 84: "The Early Years"

Early 1979, Dallas

The 74 AMF Chopper would stay in this newest version now for a whole whoppin' entire,…year. This is the version I rode cross country in the upcoming Summer of 1979 Randal Road Trip. Then in the winter of 1979 I tore it all down again, to bare sandblasted frame and rebuilt it all over again,…including the motor and tranny which were done by ace mechanic Joe Cox this time around. I was lucky to get Joe to do it, cuz Shelby had been swamped with his own work, Shelby moved to his bigger shop out in Paradise Texas.

The next version is a plumb stunnin' show bike, with a nice clean molded frame which made my fingertips bleed sandin' the Bondo, and then professionally sprayed Black Imron Paint. It turned out great, if I don't mind sayin' so my own damn self,…which I don't, wink, wink.

And yes, I still ride this same 74 AMF Chopper today, 48 years now, but it looks much different since it has been through even more rebuilds. If you have back issues of Easyriders magazines, you can find the 74 AMF Chopper in there, spread out like a sleezy hooker on 6 seedy and glorious pages in the August 1993 issue.

As for the Corvette Front, what goes around comes around. Since I had been guilty of wrecking a perfectly good 1968 Big Block Corvette which would cost a small fortune today, it was only fitting for me to deserve a rebuilt wreck to drive. Hal ran Hal's Auto Craft in Grand Prairie Texas and he built up this beautiful custom White Corvette for his wife. It was created from two other Corvettes. It also won Best Single Color Paint at the Dallas Autorama-World of Wheels. Hal took a chassis from a 1975 that had seen a few miles on it. And he got the wreckage from a brand new 1978 Corvette Pace Car that some dummy like me had totaled with less than 2,000 miles on it.

He took the engine, tranny, rear end, wheels, and black leather interior from the '78 and grafted them onto the 75 body. Then he took off those ugly rubber bumpers and stuck Eckler's one piece fiberglass units on. The he added the Pace Car spoilers front and back and topped it off with an Ecklers Moon Roof, which was sort of a brand new thing at that time. Then he sprayed the entire custom Vette in Ermine White Lacquer and did it up with Pace Car Pinstripes. Only thing was, since it had no bumpers now, it was like driving a big egg. One little bump and it woulda cracked like an egg shell. And his wife was kinda short and couldn't see over the hood good enough to park it. She was scared to drive it, so he put it up for sale and I got it.

And that brings us to early 1979 which is also the ending for this book. And if this gibberish hasn't bored you to tears and you wanna see what happens next in the on-goin' life of the 74 AMF Chopper, you can pick up "Chopper Hobo" which covers all the action from Summer of 1979 to March 1983. That book features many more road trips, runs, crashes, builds, the 74 AMF has the backbone of its frame break outside Portland Oregon, you name it, and it probably happens in that book. Plus, as an added bonus, I went broke and lost everything including this White Vette and was also homeless on the 74 AMF for 18 months and took semi-glorious photos along the tiresome and sometimes funny journey. If you desire wretched horrible stories fulla terror or enjoy nice happy sagas, "Chopper Hobo" has it all. This has been a dreadfully sleezy and shameless plug.

The End

Bonus Pages

Shelby Magazine Article and Trivia

This is Shelby, my Chopper Guru, and his Classic 1939 ULH Flathead 80 incher. And this is what Shelby and his UL both looked like when I was allowed to ride with him, cuz I was the snot nosed hang-a-round kid, 20 years old building up my first 1974 AMF Bowling Ball Shovelhead Chopper with Shelby's gracious input. He didn't hafta tell me nuthin',…but he did. He shared his knowledge with this then-inquisitive kid. Little did he know I'd still be showing him my gratitude nearly 50 years later. There is only one Shelby.

This Flathead 80 equipped with the vintage speed parts from back in the day right here is Shelby's main ride, and yes, he still has it today. This Flattie Chopper had the first open Phase 3 Belt Drive set up I ever saw, suicide clutch and jockey shift. Old classic choppers just don't come any kooler than this. And you shoulda heard them long dual fishtails spittin' out the 80 inch Flathead notes. I did. I was lucky enough that I got to ride along next to this beast from the ancient past. Shelby rode his wonderful creation everywhere and has been, and still is, a regular at Daytona Bike Week and Fandango in Texas, and him and Gloria are still together. Don't ya just love happy endings? I know I do.

Early photo of Shelby on his ultra rare Green Shriners 45. Harley only made a few of those special bikes, just for the Shriners. All production 45s had springer front ends except this special run with the glide front ends. The other chopper with the extended springer is a 45 Shelby built and that is his Trike Project build in the other photo.

SHOVELHEAD DAVE

As a matter of fact, it was Shelby who got me hooked up with a nice used 1971 D&D Jammer rigid frame, which I still ride the back end of today. The neck has been re-cut twice over the decades, but the original back section is still there. And it was Shelby who taught me what I know about building choppers. I owe it all to him and the guys he rode with, Harold, Stan, Blue, Dutch, Dangerous George, Bill, Terry, and the rest.

THE EARLY YEARS

Shelby's 220 tons of Spares

Part 1: The November 1978 issue of Custom Bike Magazine was a very special issue. Check out that lead-in line on the top of the cover. "220 Tons of H-D Treasures Discovered in Desert" That was Stubbs Wendall's fine stash, and since they were good ol' Flathead pals, Mister Shelby Withrow, Proprietor of Mid Cities Choppers in the Dallas Fort Worth area, bought it all from Stubb's widow. I think it was 17 semi trucks in total that showed up fulla the old Harley and WW 2 artifacts, if I remember right? And luckily, I was there that day to help unload it. I remember grabbin' the old US Army crates with Flathead engines in them, transmissions, engines, fenders, frames, gas tanks, oil tanks, you name it, if it went on an old Harley Davidson motorcycle, it was in this cache,…in spades. I've never seen such a haul since then,…44 years ago.

SHOVELHEAD DAVE

Part 2: Custom Bike Magazine, November 1978 Issue

Does this page of artwork get you a little bit interested?

Part 3: Custom Bike Magazine, November 1978 Issue

Dreaming of Such Things as Malibu Beachhouses, Wine, Numbers and Scanty-Clad Ronstadts: The Only Thing Within Reach Now Is the Wine... But Just You Wait!

WISHING OURSELVES WEALTHY

Things like this are fun to hear about. It's the stuff wishes are made of. When we're alone, maybe quietly working on a cold jug of Gallo Chablis and listening to Linda Ronstadt singing about "Poor, Poor, Pitiful Me," we tend to trip out on things that might have been if circumstances had been just a little bit different. We wonder, we wish, what it would be like if only the power people would take your ideas seriously. If only you hadn't been drafted. (Remember that haunting, dreaded draft? Ha, how can you forget?) If only you had spoken up when that dippy foreman started screwing things up at the shop.

If only, if only...

If only things were just a little different, you'd be hearing Ronstadt singing lusty songs to you in person as she brings you another number, then lightly slinks in her luscious altogether from the bedroom of your Malibu beach house to the kitchen, then returns with another tumbler of wine. Her delicate bare feet barely gliding across the floor. Her body a joy to watch, to experience...

Ah, (sigh) if only...

Wishes are what keep us average grunts going. Wishes are our motivation. We wish for pleasure, but end up busting our butts to achieve just a little comfort. We wish for wealth, while our wearying struggles usually yield just enough loot to maintain, but with precious little left over.

But what about quiz shows? What about lotteries and Vegas? People make big scores under those circumstances regularly, or so it seems.

And how they score! Lottery winners, for example, can you imagine receiving 50 grand a year for the rest of your life?

We can't either...

Big scores and windfalls of cosmic proportions happen to *other* people. Never *us*.

But still we keep on wishing.

To many readers, the glorious treasure that came to Shelby Withrow easily equals in magnitude the pipe(!)dreams that some motorcyclists are known to indulge in.

The following article details Shelby Withrow's experience with such a windfall experience. However, Withrow's joy in coming upon the treasure trove was tempered by grief over the death of his old friend, which also serves to remind us that we live in The Real World, not the pleasure-saturated fantasyland that exists only between our ears.
—Mike Griffin

Photos by Jill Pritchett and Gwyn Viers

Treasure Is Treasure. Whether or Not You Find It at the End of a Rainbow Means Not a Thing

by Tom Morton

Just about every biker in the country has at one time or another heard stories about Harley-Davidson Military 45 motorcycles that had been stored in crates and sold at ridiculously low prices.

The truth of the matter is the last big government auctions of military war surplus parts were held in Atlanta, Georgia, between 1954 and 1956. One of the buyers at an auction was a Harley-Davidson dealer from East Texas. He put a bid on most everything and came away from the auction with a lot of truck and aircraft parts. But

Continued on page 20

SHOVELHEAD DAVE

Part 4: Custom Bike Magazine, November 1978 Issue

mostly he bought war surplus Harley-Davidson military 45 motorcycles and parts. The old dealer who had originally purchased them at the government auction and his brother spent several months hauling motorcycle parts from Atlanta back to Texas and storing them. That is how the last big stash of military war surplus Harley-Davidson 45 parts came out to the Piney Woods of East Texas.

They stored them in some pretty unlikely places. Some parts were stored in metal buildings, others in old houses, and some were just stacked under trees with tarps thrown over them in the crates.

The beneficent old enthusiast kept his dealership going until 1962. When he closed it up, he took everything off the shelves, put it in boxes and moved his whole Harley-Davidson shop and parts into a new building near his stash of military 45 Harley-Davidson parts.

When 1977 came around, the big stash of Harley-Davidson military 45 parts had been in storage for just over 20 years. One day the old dealer's health gave out on him. He succumbed, leaving his motorcycling treasures to his estate. Prior to his death, however, he had made it clear to his family he wanted his collection and stash to go to someone who would keep his lifelong work together. And, importantly, he stipulated that the parts would not be sold off piecemeal.

Shelby Withrow, President of Texas H-D Distributors, had been a friend of the old dealer for years and regularly made 300-mile round trips to visit

Part 5: Custom Bike Magazine, November 1978 Issue

him. Over a number of years they built up a great respect for each other, both business and personal. In addition, both were Harley-Davidson collectors and enthusiasts. It was his wish Shelby should get first crack at buying the parts. The negotiations for the sale of the parts were concluded a few months after the old dealer's death and Texas H-D Distributors bought them from the old man's estate.

Buying 220 tons of motorcycle parts is one thing, moving them is another. Especially, when the weather is over 100 degrees with about 100 percent humidity. The fields where the parts were stored had not been trimmed or cut in more than 20 years and the East Texas woods had grown heavy with vines and brush. The growth in the middle of fields was over seven feet high. A trail had to be cut to get a truck in and out. Scattered in heaps under rotting tarps were the parts. Enough 45 parts to build many, many complete motorcycles. The treasure trove of parts included everything you might

Part 6: Custom Bike Magazine, November 1978 Issue

THE LATE, GREAT 80

Happiness To Shelby Withrow Is a Long-Legged Side-Valver

Shelby Withrow admits to being a custom bike traditionalist. He has very little enthusiasm for such custom movements as the Northwestern states' low-rider and related trends. No sir-ree. To Shelby, such motorcycles represent discomfort and impracticality. Withrow's passion, you see, is toward large-displacement, long-touring fat-bobs, which are as much a part of the Texas ethic as the late Bob Wills and Lone Star beer.

Although Withrow owns several motorcycles, his highway-going favorite is this 80-cu.-in. Harley-Davidson flathead.

The engine began life as a 1939 model ULH. But it's far from being a stocker. The cylinders are those hard-to-find flat-track units that were made for racing long before the current AMA class-C rules came into effect. H-D flat-track racing cams are also used, as well as lightened flywheels, high-compression heads and an Andrews Phase III primary drive.

Overall gearing is well suited to the Texas vastness, with the machine capable of attaining 96 mph in third gear. Withrow has yet to achieve an accurate clocking on the bike WFO in top gear, although he says that it peaks at about 4200 rpm in fourth. Fuel economy with the 8.5:1 powerplant is excellent: about 50 mpg!

Accurately reflecting Withrow's philosophy, there is nothing cubby about the bike, nothing radical. Just steady, reliable performance.

need, except for a few perishable items that had not been packed to protect them from the weather. The first load of stash moved consisted of mostly brand new Military 45 Harley-Davidson cylinders, both fronts and rears. They were packed three to a crate, each crate weighing about 92 pounds. The cylinders had been stored in a metal building whose only occupants were some big black wasps who had moved in during the 20 years the cylinders had been there.

The second load was mostly springer front ends that were stored in an old house where the weight of the stack of the springers had just crunched the floor right down into the earth.

Brand new 45 frames were stacked in the middle of a field under a big old tree where several more nests of wasps lived. They weren't any nicer than the ones living in the metal building. Indeed, it was soon discovered that you can move pretty fast carrying a 45 frame if you have to. Fenders were stacked around and behind an old chicken coop. Many of them were still wrapped in the original paper and in new condition. There were motors still bolted in the crates, ditto old but untouched transmissions still in the crates, brand new front and rear wheels and a small mountain of gas tanks.

But that was not all. The complete inventory of the Harley-Davidson dealership he had closed in 1962 was still in its original packing.

Then there was the old dealer's personal collection of parts from the late 1920s thru the middle 1960s. It took five months to move it, hauling two loads a weekend. Moreover, there were many exotic old parts, including an extremely rare 1936 61-cu.-in. Model EL that was technologically the beginning of the Harley-Davidson engine as we know it today. Shelby immediately reserved for his collection a rare 1936 VLH flathead motor, since his everyday transportation is a 1939 ULH flathead.

It's certainly what the old dealer would have wanted: to see all the parts kept in one place in the hands of a dedicated Harley-Davidson collector and enthusiast, because that's exactly where he wanted them to go. Shelby can be reached at Texas H-D Distributors, 3201 Pioneer Parkway East, Suite 47, Arlington, Texas, 76010. ●

"The Water Wheel"

I'd be willin' to bet that there probably ain't that many livin' souls on this planet that can claim they actually built a 19th Century-type water wheel. In the spring of 1975 just before the 1975 Road Trip with Brudder Charles and Cuzzin Johnny, I was doing some woodwork jobs in Six Flags Over Texas amusement park in Arlington.

We'd do repair work on the roller coaster arms, make new standing billboard signs, you name it, if it was wood and if it was in Six Flags, we were probably fixing it. I was 20 years old. I was working with my dad on this project and two other older carpenters who were from Fort Worth. So the four of us built this magnificent monstrosity and I am now the only one livin' to tell its story. So here we go.

Our boss was one of the nicest guys I ever worked for, a smart and funny Irishman named Pat Yeary. After my dad and I had been working for two weeks there, we got our first paper paycheck on Friday. There was a huge mistake on my check. Pat was accidentally payin' me Journeyman Wages, not the Second Year Apprentice Pay I shoulda got. When I told Pat about the mistake, he laughed and said "Ya fooled me, son. You're a big guy and you do a Journeyman's work, so it's fine with me" and he slapped me on my back. And that's how Pat was, paying me double what I shoulda been gettin'.

Now on to the water wheel. We cleared out a big area on the shop floor by moving some ancient 1920s woodworking machinery around. Most of the tools in this shop were old Chicago Tool Company tools, heavy cast iron and steel saws, shapers, band saws, drill presses, and other machines. We finally got the spot cleared out big enough. For starters, they had me drill a 1/8th inch hole in the center of the concrete floor and then I hammered a double headed 16 penny nail with a wire next to it down into the hole and I sprayed that nail head bright orange so we'd always see it and not kick it or trip over it while it was sticking up there like the trip hazard it was.

Next we got out string lines and long tape measures and, going off that nail head sticking up outta the floor in the center, we swung a circle 22 feet in diameter if my memory is correct. Then we drew in the spokes for the wheel. We built the first side down on the floor. The water wheel was made outta 6" X 6" cedar for the spokes, just like they did a hunnerd years before. Everything was being bolted together with malleable iron washers, bolts and nuts.

After we got the first side cut and assembled, which took a coupla days, we laid them aside in pie shaped pieces on the other side of the shop floor and started in on the other side. After it was about half way finished, my dad and me split off from the other two guys and we started in making the axle bearings for this creation. The axle was gonna be a pipe with big flanges welded to it. And we needed some ultra strong heavy duty old timey bearings for this thing to turn on,…right?

So they got us a big chunk of 12" X 12" solid oak. Heavy shit, for sure. As they said in the shop, "That takes two men and a boy just to lift it." My dad started in on the bearings with me helping, and he laid out the spot we were to cut.

We had to man-handle the four foot chunk up onto an old timey band saw. Now if any OSHA inspector saw this old band saw today, he'd pull up his skirt, scream, shit his pants and pass out, bwahaha! I'm talking about an old 1920s Chicago Tool Company Band Saw, one with two spoked steel wheels on it maybe 3 feet in diameter with an open saw blade running it. No guards, no safety shit on it, no nuthin', just two big wheels spinning ever so slowly with ultra sharp shark's teeth for a blade. That sucker would probably cut off your hand in less than one second.

We stuck that big ass chunk of 12" X 12" oak up on the band saw table and started in cuttin' the radiused half moon shaped spot for the axle to rest. It seemed like it took forever. Imagine cutting through 12 inches of solid oak? But it finally got cut all the way through. And then? We had to do the other chunk for the other side, hahaha. We eventually got it cut. Success, finally.

THE EARLY YEARS

Meanwhile, the other two guys were now finished with the wheel sections. We did all of this over a weekend, too, before the park was open to the public for the summer. So this was Saturday and Sunday work, which was time & half and double time back then. Money was no object, just get it done for the people, hah.

So the Sunday morning came to haul the sections down to the Music Mill itself. Now the Music Mill is/was (if they still have it?) a big outdoor amphitheater. The crowd would sit on concentric radiused seats going up the hill, and then they could look down into the Music Mill and see the bands playing there on the stage. The Music Mill itself looked like an old timey grain mill you mighta seen up in the mountains in New Mexico or Colorado 150 years ago, with the big ass 22 foot diameter water wheel turning ever so slowly off to the side.

We got the pie shaped pieces of the water wheel loaded into a bunch of pick up trucks and a flat bed trailer and we drove in a convoy through the park down to the Music Mill. They had a little crane there waiting for us. The stand and supports for the bearings were already in place, they'd had some Ironworkers doing that part. So the first thing we did was anchor those 12" X 12" oak bearings into place…solid. They can never move…ever.

Next, the crane lifted the first pie shaped piece of water wheel into place and we bolted it to the flange on the axle. Then we did the next piece, so now there's two pie shaped pieces of the water wheel up and they are bolted to each other and to the axle flanges. And this is where I became Hamster Boy. Since I was the biggest and heaviest guy there on the crew, they needed me for some Dumb Weight, hah. So I climbed up inside the two pie shaped pieces, stood on the water wheel's paddle pieces, and my weight would move the sections down to the bottom, so the crane could lift the next piece up and the guys would bolt it together in place. Then I'd be Hamster Boy and walk inside the wheel and make it turn down to the bottom so they could do the next piece…get it? I was like the hamster running in the hamster cage's wheel. So we kept that up until the entire wheel was assembled. Yay!

And then it was time for,… The Torture Test. Let's see if the damn thing actually works.

A pipe maybe 3 inches in diameter was hidden several feet way back inside the trough for the water flume. The idea was to turn on the water pipe and the water would run outta the pipe, but by the time it got to the water wheel part, it looked like a regular water flume flowin' from a mountain stream, see? It looked real. And once the water hit the water wheel's paddles, it started turning oh so slowly. And then once it made 2 or 3 revolutions and got all soakin' wet, that sucker started creakin' and groanin' just like it was 150 years old, the job was a smashing success, No issues.

Now for the Even Better Part. All the speakers and sound system stuff was up high in the rafters in the Music Mill. I was the guy who got to staple all the fabric over the speakers and I had to double check everything, to make sure nuthin' was loose to where it might fall on a band member.

And then? It got even better. I actually got paid OVERTIME to go hang out up in the rafters with my tools and watch the first two nights' bands, which were Kris Kristofferson and Chuck Berry.

And as far as I know, this is the only photo of the Six Flags Music Mill Water Wheel being built back in the spring of 1975.

THE END

OTHER BOOKS IN THIS SERIES BY SHOVELHEAD DAVE

1. The Early Years
2. Chopper Hobo
3. The California Rat Years (release date Autumn 2022)

Future books to come late 2022 and 2023

4. Building the Show Chopper

If you haven't read Chopper Hobo, here is what Jay Jay Solari had to say about it.

This is the first synopsis probably in history of an American biker adventurer with no attitude, no club affiliation telling the story of a lone youth on a Harley on an exploratory adventure to see the West on two wheels without a windshield with a can-do cheery self confidence, with no experience and learning things the hard way, with no tedious nuts-and-bolts lectures on motorcycle parts other than how to deal with problems when you have no access to help and basically every day hurling yourself in the void of the American West, one new and different day at a time and laughing at the endless hassles. Oh, and no fairing. bugs, rocks, gravel, rain and cops be damned, do your worst, this is fucking fun as hell. that's what this is. it's one of a kind. it's Huck fucking Finn on a Harley. When NOBODY who lived like this was considered worth having anything to do with at the time. Which is why these types clubbed-up. But to some even that was too regimented and this was all about freedom and "ok, what's next?? woo hoo of the TRULY hard core variety: hard core enthusiasm.

He's still at it apparently.

www.ingramcontent.com/pod-product-compliance
Lightning Source LLC
Chambersburg PA
CBHW071017240426
43661CB00073B/2357